ANCESTRAL SHADOWS

ANCESTRAL SHADOWS

UNRAVELING THE HIDDEN IMPACT OF INHERITED
FAMILY TRAUMA AND THE PATH TO RECOVERY

GENERATIONAL HEALING
BOOK 1

ESSIE WOODARD

Book Bound
STUDIOS

This book is dedicated to the brave souls who dare to explore the depths of their histories and the strength of their spirits. May the journey through these pages offer understanding, solace, and a path toward healing the wounds carried across generations. Together, we embrace the echoes of our ancestors, transforming their legacy into a beacon of hope for the future.

Healing is a matter of time, but it is sometimes also a matter of opportunity.

— HIPPOCRATES

CONTENTS

THE ECHOES OF OUR ANCESTORS

Unveiling the Legacy of the Past

In the stillness of our private moments, we often find ourselves grappling with emotions and fears that seem to have been with us longer than our memories can account for. Within the intricate tapestry of our family history, we may find the threads of these unaccounted feelings—strands of inherited family trauma that have been woven into our being across generations.

The concept of inherited family trauma is not merely a metaphor for the shared experiences within a family lineage. It is a phenomenon that has garnered attention from psychologists, geneticists, and sociologists alike. It suggests that the traumas of our forebears—the wars they waged, the losses they suffered, the adversities they overcame—do not perish with them. Instead, these experiences can leave an indelible mark on the psyche and even the genetic makeup of subsequent generations.

As we embark on this journey of understanding, it is essential to acknowledge the complexity of trauma. Trauma is not a singular event but a cascade of responses that ripple through one's life, often surfacing unexpectedly. It can manifest as a heightened state of anxiety, a predisposition to depression, or an inexplicable sense of grief. We look to the past for their origins when these symptoms arise without a direct cause.

The legacy of the past is only sometimes visible. Like the roots of a tree, it stretches deep and wide, hidden beneath the surface. Only through the careful excavation of family stories, patterns, and behaviors can we begin to unearth the impact of what has been passed down to us. This legacy can be a source of strength, imbuing us with resilience and wisdom. Yet, it can also be a burden, a silent weight we carry, often without realizing its source.

In the following pages, we will delve into the heart of what defines inherited family trauma. We will explore the mechanisms through which trauma is transmitted, the signs that suggest its presence, and how we can confront and heal from these inherited wounds. The journey requires courage and vulnerability, which involves confronting the shadows of our family's past. Yet, through this confrontation, we can emerge with a deeper understanding of ourselves and a renewed capacity for healing and growth.

As we stand on the precipice of this exploration, let us do so with empathy for those who came before us and with a commitment to breaking the cycles that may have held us back. The echoes of our ancestors carry with them stories of pain and perseverance, and it is our task to listen, learn, and liberate ourselves from the silent repercussions of their experiences.

Defining Inherited Family Trauma

At its core, inherited family trauma refers to the transference of emotional and psychological consequences from one generation to the next. This transmission is not merely about the retelling of stories or the conscious emulation of behaviors; it is an enigmatic process by which the unresolved traumas of our forebears—be they wrought by war, displacement, loss, or abuse—echo within us, influencing our behaviors, our relationships, and even our health.

The concept of inherited trauma suggests that the experiences of our ancestors can leave an imprint on the genetic material they pass down to us. This concept challenges the traditional boundaries of what we consider heritable. It is not just the color of our eyes or the shape of our nose that we inherit from our parents and their parents before them; we may also inherit a propensity for anxiety, an inclination toward specific fears, or a susceptibility to depression.

This inheritance is not one of conscious choice. Children do not select which traits or burdens they receive, nor do parents intentionally bestow their unresolved pains upon their offspring. Yet, the emotional legacies of those who came before us can be as much a part of our inheritance as the physical attributes we see in the mirror.

Inherited family trauma is not a deterministic sentence, however. Recognizing its presence is the first step toward healing and transformation. By bringing these inherited patterns into the light of awareness, we can understand their influence and, with compassion and courage, work to resolve the pain unwittingly passed down through the generations.

As we delve deeper into this exploration, we will uncover the intricate ways these traumas are transmitted and the profound implications they hold for our understanding of self, relationships with others, and collective well-being. With each step on this journey, we strive to honor the experiences of those who came before us, not as a burden but as a call to healing and growth for ourselves and future generations.

The Science of Transmission

The concept of inherited family trauma hinges on the understanding that the emotional and psychological scars of one generation can be passed down to the next, not merely through the stories shared at the dinner table, but through a more silent and pervasive medium: our very biology.

The science of transmission, in the context of inherited family trauma, is a relatively new frontier that straddles the realms of genetics, psychology, and neurobiology. It is a field that seeks to unravel the complex mechanisms by which the effects of trauma are transmitted across generations. To comprehend this phenomenon, we must delve into the realm of epigenetics, a branch of science that studies how the expression of genes can be altered without changing the genetic code itself.

Epigenetics has illuminated that environmental factors, including trauma, can lead to chemical modifications around the genes. These modifications can affect how genes are turned on or off, and remarkably, some of these epigenetic changes can be passed down to offspring. This means that the child of a person who has experienced profound trauma might inherit a predisposition for specific stress responses, even if the child does not directly experience the trauma itself.

Moreover, the transmission of trauma can also occur through learned behaviors and patterns within the family. Children often learn how to respond to the world around them by observing their parents. If a parent has developed certain behaviors as a result of trauma—such as hypervigilance, anxiety, or avoidance—these behaviors can become the blueprint for the child's responses to stress and adversity.

The interplay between these inherited epigenetic changes and learned behaviors creates a complex web of influences that can shape an individual's emotional landscape. It is a silent legacy that can manifest subtly yet profoundly, from heightened stress responses to how one navigates relationships and copes with challenges.

Understanding the science of transmission is not just an academic exercise; it carries profound implications for therapy and healing. By recognizing that the echoes of our ancestors' experiences may reverberate within us, we can begin to unravel these threads and seek to heal not only ourselves but potentially prevent the perpetuation of trauma in future generations.

As we continue to explore the depths of inherited family trauma, it is essential to consider the historical contexts that have shaped the collective experiences of entire populations. The traumas of war, displacement, and oppression do not fade with time; instead, they can leave an indelible mark on the descendants of those who directly endured such hardships. Within this broader historical framework, we can further understand the individual narratives of inherited trauma and the resilience that often emerges in the face of such enduring legacies.

Historical Contexts of Inherited Trauma

As we delve into the historical contexts of inherited trauma, we begin to understand that the experiences of our ancestors are not merely relics of the past but are intricately linked to our present lives. The notion that the emotional and psychological scars of one generation can imprint themselves onto the next is a concept that has gained increasing recognition and understanding.

To comprehend the full impact of inherited trauma, we must first acknowledge the myriad events that have left indelible marks on entire populations. Wars, genocides, slavery, and natural disasters are but a few cataclysmic occurrences that have shaped the collective psyche of affected groups. The suffering endured by those who lived through such harrowing times does not simply vanish with their passing. Instead, the effects can ripple through generations, manifesting in many ways, from psychological predispositions to behavioral patterns.

Consider, for example, the descendants of those who survived the Holocaust. Research has shown that the children and even grandchildren of survivors often carry with them an unconscious legacy of fear, anxiety, and vigilance despite never having encountered such threats themselves.

Similarly, the offspring of those who have been subjected to the brutality of slavery may inherit a deep-seated wariness and mistrust, a survival mechanism once necessary for their ancestors' very existence.

The historical contexts of inherited trauma are not limited to these large-scale atrocities. Personal and familial traumas, such as domestic violence, abuse, or the sudden loss of a loved one, can also imprint upon the family narrative. These private agonies, though perhaps not as widely acknowledged, can be just as potent in their ability to shape the lives of future generations.

It is essential to recognize that the transmission of trauma is not a simple cause-and-effect process. It is a complex interplay of genetic, environmental, social, and cultural factors. How trauma is expressed and processed—or not processed—within a family or community can significantly influence how it is carried forward. The silence around suffering, for instance, can create an environment where the pain is internalized, and its expression is stifled, leaving subsequent generations to grapple with unspoken legacies.

As we consider the historical contexts of inherited trauma, we also begin to see the resilience that is passed down alongside the pain. Stories of survival, overcoming, and strength in the face of adversity are also part of the legacy handed down. These narratives of resilience are crucial, for they offer hope and a pathway toward healing. They remind us that while the past cannot be changed, the future is unwritten, and there is power in acknowledging and addressing the echoes of our ancestors.

In this light, understanding the historical contexts of inherited trauma is not merely an academic exercise; it is a vital step in the journey toward healing. By recognizing the origins of our inherited pain, we can start to unravel the complex web of influences that shape our lives and begin the process of reclaiming our stories. This knowledge paves the way for us to approach the next steps with a sense of purpose and possibility as we seek to transform the legacy of trauma into one of understanding, growth, and renewal.

Setting the Stage for Healing

Now, as we stand at the threshold of understanding, it is time to illuminate the path toward healing. The recognition of inherited family trauma is not an end but a beginning—a point of departure from which we can embark on a transformative journey. This journey is about tracing the scars of the past and learning how to heal them in the present and prevent their perpetuation into the future.

Healing inherited trauma requires a multifaceted approach. It begins with acknowledging the pain passed down, often obscured by the mists of time. To set the stage for healing, we must first create a space of safety and acceptance where these inherited wounds can be gently revealed and explored. This space is not just physical but emotional and psychological —a sanctuary within ourselves and our communities where vulnerability is not a liability but a bridge to deeper understanding.

Empathy is the cornerstone of this healing process. It allows us to connect with our ancestors' experiences, feel the weight of their burdens, and offer them the compassion they may never have received. Through empathy, we can begin to disentangle our own identity from the legacy of trauma, recognizing that while it has shaped us, it does not define us.

Analytical reflection is equally important. It involves a careful examination of the patterns that trauma has woven into our family narratives. We can identify how these patterns have influenced our beliefs, behaviors, and relationships by understanding them. This understanding empowers us to make conscious choices about which threads we wish to carry forward and which we choose to release.

The journey of healing is not linear. It ebbs and flows, with moments of profound insight and periods of quiet growth. It requires patience, for the work of untangling generations of trauma cannot be rushed. It demands courage, for confronting the pain of the past can be daunting. And it necessitates hope—a belief in the possibility of change and the potential for renewal.

As we embark on this journey, we are not alone. We walk alongside those who have come before us, guided by their stories and strengthened by their spirit. And we walk with each other, sharing the common bond of humanity that transcends time and place.

In setting the stage for healing, we are not merely addressing the echoes of our ancestors. We are shaping the legacy we will leave for those who follow. It is a profound responsibility and a precious opportunity to weave a new pattern in the tapestry of our lineage—one that honors the past while forging a future defined by healing, resilience, and love.

THE WEBS WE WEAVE: PATTERNS OF TRAUMA

Identifying Patterns in Family Histories

The exploration of family histories is akin to the work of an archeologist, sifting through layers of time to uncover the artifacts of past traumas. These traumas, whether they be events of war, displacement, abuse, or loss, do not dissipate with the passing of those who first endured them.

Instead, they can imprint themselves upon the psyche of subsequent generations, manifesting in behaviors, beliefs, and emotional responses that seem disconnected from the immediate experiences of those who carry them.

To identify these patterns, we must first acknowledge the resilience and the suffering of those who came before us. It is a delicate balance to honor their strength while recognizing the wounds they could not heal. In doing so, we begin to see how specific themes recur: a grandparent's unspoken grief mirrored in a parent's inability to express love, or a great-aunt's experience of abandonment echoed in the pervasive loneliness of her descendants.

These patterns are not always negative; they can also be sources of strength and survival. A family's legacy of overcoming adversity may inspire courage and determination in the face of modern challenges. However, when the inherited patterns are maladaptive, they can lead to a cycle of pain that perpetuates until acknowledged and addressed.

We must approach our family histories with empathy and a critical eye in identifying these patterns. We must listen to the stories with an understanding that memory is often selective and subjective. We must recognize the filters through which these stories are told and retold, shaped by cultural norms, personal biases, and the human tendency to create coherence out of chaos.

Through this process, we begin to map out the emotional landscape of our lineage. We may discover that a tendency towards anxiety is not simply a personal challenge but a thread that has run through our family for generations. Or we may find that our difficulty with trust and intimacy is not an isolated struggle but part of a broader familial pattern of insecure attachments.

As we chart these patterns, we prepare the ground for the work of healing. We can start to untangle the webs woven through our families by bringing these inherited traumas into the light. We can begin to differentiate which parts of our emotional inheritance are ours to carry and which we can lay down, breaking the cycle for ourselves and future generations.

This work is not done in isolation. In the context of our relationships

—those intimate attachments that shape our lives—we often find the most apparent reflections of our inherited traumas and the most significant opportunities for healing. Within the crucible of connection, we can confront and transform the legacies of the past, forging new patterns that will become the inheritance of those who follow.

The Role of Attachment and Relationships

In the intricate dance of human development, the earliest steps are often taken hand-in-hand with our primary caregivers. Within these formative relationships, the seeds of our future selves are sown, for better or worse. The attachment styles we develop as infants and children can become the templates for future relationships, influencing how we connect with others, manage emotional stress, and perceive the world around us. When these early bonds are disrupted by trauma, the reverberations can echo through generations.

Trauma, in its most insidious form, can infiltrate the nurturing bonds between parent and child. A parent's unresolved trauma can manifest as emotional unavailability, inconsistency, or even direct maltreatment. In their profound adaptability and need for attachment, children may internalize these patterns, misunderstanding them as reflections of their worth. They may grow to associate love with pain, care with unpredictability, and intimacy with danger. This internalized narrative can profoundly shape their emotional landscape, guiding them, often unconsciously, in their future relationships.

The transmission of trauma is not merely a psychological phenomenon. Still, it is also rooted in the biological processes that underpin our stress responses. When a child is exposed to a traumatic environment, their developing brain adapts to this heightened state of alert. These adaptations can be life-saving in the short term. Still, they may lead to long-term dysregulation of the body's stress response systems. Such dysregulation can leave an individual more vulnerable to mental health challenges. It can even influence the way they parent their children, thus perpetuating the cycle of trauma.

However, the story of attachment and relationships within the context of inherited family trauma is not one of deterministic gloom. It is also a testament to the resilience of the human spirit and the malleability of our relational blueprints. Secure attachments, whether formed in early childhood or developed through later reparative relationships, can offer a powerful counter-narrative to trauma. They can provide a sense of safety that allows for the exploration of vulnerability, the reevaluation of self-worth, and the gradual healing of old wounds.

Therapeutic interventions, supportive relationships, and sometimes even the simple passage of time can contribute to reshaping attachment styles. The recognition and processing of inherited trauma can lead to a conscious uncoupling from destructive patterns. This journey towards healing is not linear nor straightforward, but it is possible. It requires a compassionate understanding of one's history and an unwavering commitment to forging a different path.

As we navigate the complexities of our relationships, we must acknowledge the profound impact our earliest attachments have on our lives. By understanding the role of these attachments in the perpetuation of family trauma, we can begin to unravel the webs we have woven. Through this understanding, we can seek to create new patterns, not only for ourselves but for the generations that follow. In the next breath of our exploration, we will delve into the generational cycles of trauma, examining how repetition and variation play out across the tapestry of time.

Generational Cycles: Repetition and Variation

In the intricate dance of family dynamics, the steps are often choreographed by the silent music of the past. As we delve into the generational cycles of inherited family trauma, we observe a complex interplay of repetition and variation. This pattern is as revealing as it is enigmatic.

Trauma, by its very nature, is a rupture—a profound disruption in the fabric of one's experience of safety, connection, and identity. When such a rupture occurs, it does not heal with time alone. Instead, it often leaves an indelible mark, not just on the individual who experienced it but also on the tapestry of their lineage. This mark can manifest as a pattern of behavior, an emotional response, or even a physiological reaction, passed down through generations, sometimes subtly, sometimes with the force of a tidal wave.

The repetition in these generational cycles can be seen in the recurrence of specific traumas within a family. Abuse, neglect, addiction, and violence are among the many forms of suffering that can become a legacy, handed down as if they were a family heirloom. Children born into environments where these patterns are the norm may grow to replicate the behaviors and coping mechanisms they observed in their parents and grandparents. The repetition is not merely a mimicry; it is often an unconscious enactment of unresolved pain.

Yet, within these cycles, there is also variation. No two individuals experience trauma in precisely the same way. Thus, how trauma is expressed and carried forward can differ significantly. One sibling may internalize the trauma, leading to a life marked by depression and self-doubt. At the same time, another may externalize it, becoming aggressive or engaging in risky behaviors. These variations are influenced by many factors, including personality, resilience, social support, and even the unique combination of genes inherited from one's ancestors.

Understanding these cycles requires a deep empathy for how trauma can shape a life. It calls for an analytical eye that can discern patterns often hidden in plain sight, woven into the daily lives of those affected. It also demands recognizing the strength and resilience that can emerge from such hardship. Within these generational cycles, there is also the potential for healing and transformation.

As we consider the role of attachment and relationships in the previous section, we recognize that the bonds formed between parent and child can either perpetuate the cycle of trauma or become the crucible for its resolution. The quality of these relationships often dictates the trajectory of the cycle, determining whether the repetition of trauma will be a curse or a challenge to overcome.

The path to breaking these cycles is difficult, as it often involves confronting painful truths and challenging deeply ingrained behaviors. Yet, it is a path that holds the promise of liberation—not just for the individual but for the generations that follow. In the next section, we will explore the burden of silence and secrecy that often accompanies family trauma and how breaking this silence can be a decisive step toward healing.

The Burden of Silence and Secrecy

Within family history, threads of silence and secrecy often run deep, weaving patterns that are as complex as they are concealed. The burden of these unspoken legacies can weigh heavily on the shoulders of subsequent generations, manifesting in subtle and profound ways.

Silence, in the context of inherited family trauma, is not merely the absence of dialogue; it is a presence, a force that shapes the contours of family life. It can be a protective measure, a shield raised to guard against the pain of past experiences. Yet, this silence often comes at a cost. It can create a vacuum where understanding and empathy might otherwise flourish, leaving individuals to grapple with the shadows of trauma without the solace of shared recognition or the guidance of narrative.

Secrecy, too, serves as a coping mechanism, a barrier erected to keep the outside world at bay. It is the keeper of stories that are too painful, shameful, or feared to be exposed to the light of day. But secrecy can also be a source of isolation. This wall separates family members and their histories from each other. The secrets we keep are not inert; they have the power to shape identities, influence relationships, and dictate behaviors.

The consequences of this silence and secrecy are not confined to the emotional and psychological realm. They can ripple through the very fabric of family life, affecting communication, trust, and the ability to form healthy attachments. Children raised in the shadow of unspoken trauma may learn to read the unarticulated cues of their caregivers, becoming hyper-vigilant or emotionally guarded as a result. They may need to understand their origins and costs to carry these adaptive behaviors into adulthood.

Moreover, the burden of silence and secrecy can lead to disconnection from one's heritage. Without the stories that anchor us to our past, we can feel adrift, untethered from the lineage that has, in part, shaped who we are. This disconnection can be particularly disorienting in times of personal crisis when we most need a sense of continuity and belonging.

Yet, the silence is not impenetrable, nor is the secrecy absolute. Cracks can appear in the façade, often at unexpected moments:

- A family gathering.
- A comment made in passing.
- A reaction that seems disproportionate to its cause.

These fissures can provide glimpses into the hidden chambers of family history, offering opportunities for healing and understanding.

Breaking the silence and piercing the veil of secrecy requires courage. It demands a willingness to confront painful truths and to bear witness to the suffering of those who came before us. It also requires compassion for ourselves and our ancestors, whose choices were often dictated by circumstances beyond their control.

As we navigate the complexities of inherited family trauma, we must strive to balance the need for protection with the need for revelation. In doing so, we can begin to loosen the grip of the past and transform the burden of silence and secrecy into a legacy of resilience and openness. Through this transformation, we can forge new patterns in the webs we weave, patterns that honor our history without being trapped by it.

Trauma and Identity Formation

As we delve deeper into the intricate relationship between trauma and identity formation, it is essential to recognize that the impact of inherited family trauma is not merely a footnote in the story of an individual's life; it is often a central chapter that influences the narrative arc in profound ways. Identity, the sense of self that we carry and present to the world, is a mosaic of our experiences, beliefs, and the history that precedes us. When that history includes trauma, the pieces of the mosaic can take on different shades, sometimes darker and more complex than we might have anticipated.

For many, the realization that their identity has been partly shaped by the traumas of their forebears can be unsettling. It raises questions about autonomy and free will: How much of who I am is truly mine, and how much is the legacy of pain I carry within me? This is not to say that inherited trauma dictates one's destiny or diminishes the capacity for growth and self-determination. Instead, it suggests that the journey of self-discovery must also include a journey through the past, a process of understanding and, where possible, healing.

The imprints of trauma can manifest in various aspects of identity, including the roles we adopt within our families and communities, the values we hold dear, and the coping mechanisms we develop to navigate the world. A child raised in the shadow of a parent's unspoken grief may learn to tread lightly to avoid the landmines of emotion that seem to lurk beneath the surface. Another might internalize a sense of resilience, a legacy of ancestors who survived and persevered through unimaginable hardships.

Yet, the influence of trauma on identity is not always about the direct transmission of specific behaviors or attitudes. Sometimes, it is about the absence of specific experiences or expressions. The void left by a grandparent's untold story, the silence that shrouds a family's collective pain, can create a palpable presence in one's life, a blank space on the canvas of identity that begs to be acknowledged and understood.

In grappling with how inherited trauma shapes identity, it is crucial to approach the subject with compassion for oneself and one's lineage. The process of untangling the webs of trauma is not about assigning blame or dwelling in the realm of what-ifs. It is about recognizing the strength and vulnerability that coexist within the human spirit and the capacity to carry forward the wounds and the wisdom of those who came before us.

As we move forward in our exploration of inherited family trauma, we must hold space for the complexity of identity formation, for the interplay of light and shadow that defines our personal and collective histories. In doing so, we honor not only the struggles of our ancestors but also our ongoing journey toward understanding, healing, and, ultimately, transformation.

Chapter Summary

- Family histories can reveal patterns of trauma, such as war, abuse, or loss, that affect subsequent generations through behaviors and emotional responses.
- These patterns can be harmful, perpetuating pain cycles, and positive, inspiring resilience and determination.
- Empathy and critical analysis are needed to identify these patterns, understanding that memory and storytelling are subjective and influenced by cultural and personal biases.
- Recognizing familial patterns helps differentiate which emotional traits are inherited and which can be released to break cycles of trauma.
- Early attachment styles with caregivers set templates for future relationships. They can be disrupted by trauma, affecting stress management and perception.
- Trauma is transmitted through both psychological and biological processes, influencing parenting and perpetuating cycles, but secure attachments can counteract this.
- Generational cycles of trauma involve repetition of behaviors like abuse or neglect, but also variation, as individuals respond differently based on many factors.
- Silence and secrecy in families can perpetuate trauma, but breaking this silence can lead to healing and the creation of new, healthier patterns.

THE BODY KEEPS THE SCORE: PHYSIOLOGICAL IMPACTS

The Biology of Trauma

The biology of trauma is not confined to the psychological realm; it is deeply rooted in the very physiology of our bodies, influencing the complex interplay of genes, hormones, and neural pathways.

When we consider the physiological impacts of trauma, we must acknowledge the body's initial response mechanisms. These are the acute, often life-saving reactions that occur in the face of threat: the rapid heartbeat, adrenaline surge, and heightened senses. These responses are orchestrated by the sympathetic nervous system, which acts as a mobilizing force, preparing the body for action.

However, the effects of trauma extend beyond these immediate responses. When the body is subjected to chronic stress or repeated traumatic events, the stress response system can become dysregulated. Cortisol, a hormone released in response to stress, can be chronically elevated, or levels may become blunted over time. This dysregulation can lead to various physical health problems, such as increased susceptibility to illness, inflammation, and metabolic irregularities.

Moreover, trauma can leave its mark on the brain. Neuroimaging studies have shown that exposure to trauma can lead to changes in the structure and function of the brain, particularly in areas involved in processing emotions and memory, such as the amygdala, hippocampus, and prefrontal cortex. These alterations can affect an individual's ability to regulate emotions, create and retrieve memories, and respond to future stressors.

The enduring nature of these physiological changes raises a profound question: can the impact of trauma be passed down from one generation to the next? The burgeoning field of epigenetics provides a compelling answer. Epigenetic mechanisms, such as DNA methylation, can modify the expression of genes without altering the genetic code itself. These modifications can be influenced by environmental factors, including traumatic experiences, and, crucially, they can be inherited.

Thus, the legacy of trauma is not solely a narrative of psychological scars; it is also a biological reality. The children and grandchildren of those who have suffered may inherit a predisposition to specific stress responses, even in the absence of direct exposure to trauma. This inheritance can manifest as a heightened sensitivity to stress or an increased risk for various physical and mental health conditions.

It is within this biological framework that we begin to understand the profound and far-reaching consequences of inherited family trauma. The body keeps the score, recording the echoes of past traumas in the very cells and systems that sustain life. As we delve deeper into the science of stress responses across generations, we uncover not only the mechanisms of inheritance but also the potential for healing and resilience that can disrupt the cycle of trauma.

Stress Responses Across Generations

Like a sad melody that lingers in the air long after the last note has been played, the physiological impacts of trauma can reverberate through generations, subtly influencing the stress responses of descendants.

As we delve deeper into the physiological impacts of inherited family trauma, it becomes evident that the body does, indeed, keep the score. The stress responses that were once adaptive for our ancestors, enabling them to survive threats and dangers, may become maladaptive in their offspring, manifesting in heightened states of anxiety, vigilance, or fear even in the absence of direct threats.

These inherited stress responses are not merely psychological artifacts; they are deeply rooted in the very biology of the body. Children and grandchildren of those who have endured severe trauma may find themselves with a biological inheritance that primes them for a heightened stress response. This legacy is not one of choice and is not quickly shed.

The mechanisms through which these stress responses are passed down are complex and multifaceted. They involve the stories told and behaviors learned within a family and the silent, unseen transmission of physiological changes. These changes can alter how the body responds to stress, potentially affecting heart rate, cortisol levels, and even the structure and function of the brain.

The body's stress response system, primarily the hypothalamic-pituitary-adrenal (HPA) axis, can be tuned by early life experiences to become more reactive or more restrained. This tuning can be beneficial, preparing an individual to cope with the specific challenges of their environment. However, when the environment changes or the stress response is calibrated too high or too low, it can lead to a mismatch between the individual's physiological responses and the demands of their current context.

Moreover, the body's response to stress is not only about the imme-diate adrenaline surge or cortisol release. It is also about the long-term effects these responses have on the body. Chronic activation of the stress response system can lead to wear and tear on the body, a concept known as allostatic load. As emerging research suggests, this burden can accu-mulate over a lifetime. It may be passed on to the next generation, predis-posing them to various health issues.

The implications of these findings are profound. They suggest that the work of healing from trauma is not only an individual pursuit but a generational one. It is a process that requires understanding, compassion, and a recognition of the invisible threads that connect the past, present, and future.

As we move forward, the conversation will shift to the burgeoning field of epigenetics, which offers a scientific framework for understanding how the effects of trauma can be transmitted across generations without direct changes to the DNA sequence. This field holds the promise of unraveling the complex interplay between genes and the environment, providing insights into how the legacy of trauma is carried within us and how we might begin to untangle its threads.

Epigenetics: The Interface of Genes and Environment

In the intricate dance of life, our genes choreograph a complex routine, not performed in isolation but in constant interaction with the environ-ment. This interplay, a field known as epigenetics, reveals how external factors can influence the expression of our genes without altering the genetic code itself. It is within this nuanced biological conversation that we begin to understand how the echoes of inherited family trauma may reverberate through generations.

The concept of epigenetics bridges the once-wide chasm between nature and nurture. It suggests that our behaviors, experiences, and even our ancestors' experiences can leave a molecular mark on our DNA. These marks do not change the sequence of the DNA but can affect how cells "read" genes. This means that the legacy of trauma is not only psychological but can also be biological.

Consider a family tree with roots that delve deep into soils rich with history and strife. The branches of this tree may bear the unseen scars of past generations' adversities. When a grandparent experiences trauma, the stress can lead to chemical changes in their DNA. These changes, known as epigenetic modifications, can be passed down to their children and grandchildren, influencing their susceptibility to stress and mental health disorders.

The mechanism behind this transmission is not a direct handover of traumatic memories but rather an alteration in the stress response systems. For instance, the hypothalamic-pituitary-adrenal (HPA) axis, which regulates our stress response, can be modified epigenetically, leading to heightened or muted reactions to stress. These modifications can prime the body to react to threats in a way that may have been adaptive in a traumatic environment but can be maladaptive in a safe one.

Moreover, the nurturing environment provided by parents can also have epigenetic effects. A mother's care can lead to the development of a specific type of glucocorticoid receptor in her offspring, which helps them manage stress effectively. Conversely, a lack of nurturing care can result in fewer receptors, leading to a more sensitive stress response. This illustrates how the care we receive can shape our epigenetic makeup, potentially counteracting some of the inherited modifications.

The implications of epigenetic inheritance are profound, suggesting that the work of healing from trauma is not solely psychological or individual but can also be biological and collective. It opens up new avenues for understanding how interventions, such as therapy, social support, and lifestyle changes, might not only help individuals but also have the potential to break the cycle of transmitted trauma for future generations.

As we delve deeper into the physiological impacts of inherited family trauma, we must consider the body as a vessel that carries not just the genetic blueprint passed down from our ancestors but also the subtle imprints of their experiences. The body, in its wisdom, keeps the score. Through epigenetics, we begin to decipher the scoresheet, understanding the marks left by the past as we navigate the path toward healing.

Somatic Memory and the Trauma Landscape

In the intricate tapestry of human physiology, somatic memory stands out as a profound testament to the body's capacity to remember and, in some cases, relive experiences of trauma. This phenomenon extends beyond the individual, reaching back through generations, as the echoes of ancestral pain are not solely confined to the realm of narrative and lore but are also inscribed within the human fabric of their descendants.

In its wisdom, the body often becomes a repository for the unspoken, unresolved, and unfathomable traumas courting through the bloodlines. Though not directly experienced by the individual, these traumas can manifest as somatic symptoms—physical sensations, pains, or ailments for which there is no apparent cause. It is as if the body itself becomes a landscape, marked by the topography of inherited trauma, with each physical manifestation serving as a landmark to a past that is not entirely one's own.

This landscape is not uniform; it varies from person to person, shaped by the unique interplay of genetic predisposition and environmental factors. Some may carry the weight of this legacy in their posture, a particular stoop of the shoulders as if bearing an invisible burden. Others might experience inexplicable anxieties, a heart that races at the whisper of a memory that does not belong to them, or a sudden breathlessness as if the air of a bygone era has momentarily become too thick to breathe.

The science of psychoneuroimmunology has begun to unravel the complex communication network between the mind, the nervous system, and the immune system, suggesting that the body's physiological responses can indeed be influenced by psychological trauma. This communication network is not a one-way street; it is a dynamic, bidirectional flow of information that can perpetuate a state of heightened alertness or chronic stress, often without the individual's conscious awareness.

As we delve deeper into the somatic expressions of inherited trauma, it becomes increasingly clear that these are not merely psychological phenomena cloaked in physical form. They result from a profound entanglement of the emotional and the human, where the body serves as both a sensor and a scribe, recording the silent stories of past generations.

The implications of this understanding are vast, as they challenge the traditional boundaries between mind and body, between past and present. They call for a compassionate and holistic approach to healing, acknowledging the full spectrum of inheritance that shapes our being. It is a journey that requires us to listen intently to the whispers of our bodies, honor the legacy they carry, and engage in the delicate work of untangling the threads of trauma that are woven into our very flesh and blood.

As we move forward, the exploration of how these somatic memories translate into tangible health outcomes will further illuminate the enduring impact of ancestral trauma. It will guide us in finding pathways to understand and heal the wounds that time has not erased, fostering resilience and hope for future generations.

Health Outcomes Linked to Ancestral Trauma

Research has begun to shed light on how the echoes of our forebears' hardships reverberate through time, leaving biological imprints on their descendants. Epigenetics, the study of how genes can be turned on or off by environmental factors, has provided a framework for understanding how the stress and trauma experienced by one generation can alter the genetic expression of the next. These changes do not alter the DNA sequence. Still, they can influence how genes are expressed, potentially predisposing individuals to various health conditions.

For instance, studies have shown that the children and grandchildren of individuals who have endured extreme stress, such as survivors of the Holocaust or famine, may have an increased risk for specific health issues, including metabolic disorders and mental health conditions. This suggests that the physiological stress responses shaped by trauma can be passed down, potentially priming the body to react more intensely to stressors or disrupting normal metabolic processes.

Moreover, the impact of inherited family trauma is not limited to direct physiological effects. It can also influence behaviors that contribute to health outcomes. For example, a family history of trauma may lead to patterns of coping that include substance abuse, overeating, or avoidance, which can, in turn, lead to a host of chronic health conditions, such as heart disease, obesity, and addiction.

The implications of these findings are profound, as they suggest that an individual's health cannot be fully understood without considering the historical context of their lineage. The experiences of our ancestors are inscribed in the very fabric of our being, influencing not only our susceptibility to certain diseases but also our resilience in the face of new challenges.

As we continue to unravel the mysteries of how ancestral trauma affects health, it becomes increasingly clear that the care we provide must be holistic, acknowledging the intricate interplay between our genetic heritage, our personal experiences, and the environment in which we live. It is a call to look beyond the individual to the ancestral stories that shape our health narratives and to approach healing with a compassionate and scientifically informed understanding.

In this light, the journey toward wellness becomes a personal quest and a collective endeavor to heal the wounds of the past so that future generations may be freed from the physiological burdens of unspoken histories. The body, indeed, keeps the score. Still, through awareness, research, and empathy, we can begin to settle the accounts of the past and chart a path toward a healthier future.

Chapter Summary

- The biology of trauma affects our genes, hormones, and neural pathways, with effects that can span generations.
- Trauma triggers an acute stress response orchestrated by the sympathetic nervous system, preparing the body for action.
- Chronic stress or repeated trauma can lead to dysregulation of the stress response system, causing physical health problems.

- Trauma can alter brain structures like the amygdala, hippocampus, and prefrontal cortex, affecting emotion regulation and memory.
- Epigenetics shows that trauma can lead to inheritable changes in gene expression without altering the DNA sequence itself.
- The physiological changes from trauma, including altered stress responses, can be passed down, affecting descendants' health and stress sensitivity.
- The field of epigenetics bridges nature and nurture, suggesting that experiences can leave molecular marks on DNA that influence gene expression.
- Ancestral trauma can manifest as somatic symptoms and influence health outcomes, necessitating a holistic approach to healing that considers generational impacts.

3

IN THE MIND'S EYE: PSYCHOLOGICAL CONSEQUENCES

The Psychological Imprint of Trauma

Trauma, by its very nature, is a complex beast, often casting long shadows not only over the life of the one who directly experiences it but also across the generations that follow. The psychological imprint of trauma is a profound and pervasive mark that can shape the mental landscape of descendants in ways that are both subtle and significant.

To understand the impact of inherited family trauma, it is essential to recognize that the transmission of trauma is not merely a matter of narrative inheritance, where stories of past hardships are passed down through the family lore. Instead, it is a more insidious process that can alter the very fabric of an individual's psychological makeup. This alteration can manifest in various forms, including heightened anxiety and depression, which we will explore in greater depth.

Anxiety, a state of heightened apprehension and fear, is often a typical response to trauma. When trauma is inherited, this anxiety can become a baseline state for those who carry the legacy of their forebears' suffering. It may present as a pervasive sense of unease, a constant anticipation of threat, or an inability to find comfort in the predictability of daily life. For some, this anxiety is diffuse, lacking an explicit source or trigger, making it all the more challenging to address and manage.

Depression, on the other hand, can be seen as the heavy cloak of inherited trauma. It can weigh down individuals with a sense of hopelessness, a loss of interest in life, and a pervasive sadness that seems to have no beginning or end. This form of depression is not simply a reaction to one's immediate circumstances. Still, it is often a more profound, more existential despair that echoes previous generations' unresolved grief and losses.

The mechanisms through which these psychological states are transmitted are varied and complex. They may involve behavioral patterns modeled by traumatized parents, biochemical changes resulting from stress, or even epigenetic modifications that alter how genes are expressed without changing the genetic code. These epigenetic changes can then be passed down, potentially predisposing offspring to similar psychological struggles.

It is crucial to acknowledge that the inheritance of trauma is not a destiny set in stone. Resilience, too, can be a family legacy. The recognition of these patterns is the first step toward healing. With appropriate support and intervention, individuals can learn to navigate their inherited landscapes of anxiety and depression. Through therapy, mindfulness practices, and sometimes medication, the chains of trauma can be loosened, allowing for a reclamation of agency and a path toward a more hopeful future.

As we delve further into the nuances of inherited family trauma, we will explore not only the challenges it presents but also the opportunities for growth and transformation that can arise when these deep-seated psychological imprints are brought into the light of conscious awareness.

Anxiety, Depression, and Inherited Trauma

In the labyrinth of the human psyche, the shadows of anxiety and depression often lurk, hidden yet potent. When these shadows are cast by one's own experiences and the silent legacy of ancestral pain, their grip can be particularly tenacious. Inherited family trauma, a phenomenon only recently gaining broader recognition within the psychological community, can manifest as a predisposition to these debilitating mental health conditions.

Anxiety, a state of heightened apprehension and fear, is a natural stress response. However, when this response is magnified or triggered by seemingly innocuous events, it may echo past family traumas. Individuals carrying this burden may find themselves inexplicably tense, their bodies bracing for threats that are no longer present, their minds trapped by a history they may not fully comprehend.

Similarly, depression can be a heavy cloak woven from threads of sadness, hopelessness, and fatigue. It can descend upon a person with a weight that feels both inexplicably personal and eerily foreign. For those with inherited trauma, depression may not always arise from their immediate life circumstances. Still, it may be an emotional resonance from ancestral struggles, losses, or hardships that were never fully processed or healed.

The mechanisms through which these conditions are passed down are complex and multifaceted. Epigenetics, the study of how genes can be turned on or off by environmental factors, suggests that our forebears' experiences can shape our genes' expression, potentially predisposing us to similar psychological states. Moreover, the family environment, with

23

its patterns of behavior, communication, and emotional expression, can perpetuate a legacy of anxiety and depression, teaching new generations to respond to the world in ways that mirror the unresolved traumas of the past.

It is crucial to acknowledge that while the inheritance of trauma can predispose individuals to anxiety and depression, it does not dictate destiny. The human mind possesses a remarkable capacity for resilience and healing. Understanding the origins of one's emotional landscape can be a decisive first step in the journey toward recovery. This knowledge can illuminate the path for therapeutic interventions that address the individual's current symptoms and honor and heal the wounds carried from generations past.

As we delve deeper into the psychological consequences of inherited family trauma, we must also consider the cognitive dimensions of this legacy. How thought patterns and beliefs are shaped by the silent narratives of our ancestors' experiences can profoundly influence our perceptions and reactions to the world around us. Within this intricate interplay of past and present, memory and experience, we find the keys to unlocking the patterns that bind us and the potential for transformation that lies within.

Cognitive Echoes: Thought Patterns and Beliefs

In the labyrinthine corridors of the mind, where memories and experiences intertwine, the legacy of inherited family trauma often manifests as persistent cognitive echoes that shape thought patterns and beliefs. These echoes reverberate through generations, subtly influencing the mental frameworks within which individuals operate. The psychological consequences of such inherited trauma are not merely emotional but also cognitive, affecting how one perceives the world and oneself.

The insidious nature of these cognitive echoes lies in their ability to operate below the level of conscious awareness. Individuals may find themselves harboring beliefs that are not the product of their own experiences but are instead inherited remnants of their ancestors' unprocessed traumas. These beliefs can manifest in various ways, such as a pervasive sense of danger in safe situations, an underlying feeling of unworthiness, or a tendency to expect abandonment or betrayal without cause.

Thought patterns, too, can be shaped by these inherited echoes. A person might be prone to catastrophic thinking, always anticipating the worst outcome, because their forebears lived through times when such outcomes were expected. Alternatively, one might engage in black-and-white thinking, struggling to see the nuances in situations or people, mirroring the survival mechanisms of ancestors who lived when quick, decisive judgments were necessary.

The impact of these thought patterns and beliefs is profound. They can influence one's choices and behaviors, often leading to self-fulfilling prophecies that reinforce the inherited trauma narrative. For instance, a belief in inevitable abandonment can lead to behaviors that push others away, thus perpetuating a cycle of isolation and reinforcing the belief.

Recognizing and addressing these cognitive echoes is a crucial step in healing from inherited family trauma. It requires a deep and often challenging introspection to discern which aspects of one's thought patterns and beliefs are genuinely personal and which are echoes of the past. Therapeutic interventions, such as cognitive-behavioral therapy, narrative therapy, or family systems therapy, can provide the tools to untangle these inherited threads.

Through this process, individuals can begin to rewrite the cognitive scripts handed down to them, crafting beliefs and thought patterns more congruent with their own experiences and aspirations. As they do so, they not only liberate themselves from the weight of their ancestors' unprocessed traumas but also halt the transmission of these psychological patterns to future generations.

The journey of healing from inherited family trauma is not a solitary one. It is a collective endeavor that requires compassion, understanding, and the courage to confront the shadows that linger in the mind's eye. By doing so, one can emerge with a newfound sense of agency and the ability to craft a narrative that honors the past without being trapped.

The Shadow of Trauma in Dreams and Imagination

In the quiet solitude of the night, when the conscious mind slips into the background, the subconscious takes the stage. It is here, in the realm of dreams and imagination, that the shadow of inherited family trauma often manifests most vividly. The individuals carrying this legacy may find themselves haunted by recurring nightmares or besieged by intrusive thoughts that seem to arise from a well of collective memory rather than personal experience.

In their enigmatic language, dreams often serve as the canvas upon which these inherited fears and anxieties are painted. A grandchild of war refugees might dream of fleeing an unseen enemy, the emotional residue of their grandparents' harrowing escapes embedded within their psyche. These nocturnal visions, while abstract, carry the emotional weight of the original trauma, suggesting that the experiences of our ancestors can indeed ripple through generations, influencing the deepest layers of our minds.

The imagination, too, can be a fertile ground for these inherited narratives to take root. It is not uncommon for individuals to find themselves drawn to specific themes in literature or cinema that resonate with their family's past traumas. They may feel a profound connection to stories of loss and survival without fully understanding why. This inexplicable pull towards certain narratives can be a subconscious attempt to make sense of the echoes of trauma that reside within them.

The interplay between dreams and imagination in the context of inherited family trauma is complex. Both can act as a mirror reflecting previous generations' unresolved emotions and experiences. Yet, they also provide a means for expression and processing. Through dreams, the mind attempts to reconcile the past's unresolved conflicts. At the same time, the imagination offers a space to explore and understand these inherited emotional landscapes.

It is crucial to recognize that these psychological phenomena are not merely echoes of a bygone era but are active elements in the individual's current emotional life. They can shape one's perception of the world, influence relationships, and even guide life choices. Acknowledging the presence of these inherited patterns is the first step towards under-standing their impact and integrating them into one's narrative to foster growth and healing.

As we delve deeper into the psychological consequences of inherited family trauma, we begin to see that the mind's eye—through dreams and imagination—does not merely reflect past sorrows but also holds the potential for resilience and transformation. Within this inner landscape, the seeds of coping mechanisms and the capacity for resilience are sown, allowing individuals to navigate the complexities of their inherited stories with strength and grace.

Coping Mechanisms and Resilience

As we delve deeper into the psychological landscape shaped by inherited family trauma, we find that individuals are not merely passive recipients of their ancestors' legacies. Instead, they are active participants in their psychological journey, often employing a variety of coping mechanisms to navigate the complex emotional terrain they have inherited. While diverse in form and function, these mechanisms serve as a testament to human resilience in the face of intergenerational pain.

Coping mechanisms can be as unique as the individuals who deploy them, tailored to their specific needs and circumstances. Some may find solace in the arts, using creative expression to process and externalize the emotions that simmer beneath the surface. Writing, painting, and music become conduits for unspoken feelings, releasing tension that might otherwise remain trapped within the psyche.

Others may turn to the structure and support of rituals and traditions. Often passed down through generations, these practices can provide a sense of continuity and belonging that counteracts the isolation trauma can engender. By engaging in these time-honored customs, individuals can connect with their ancestors in a way that is both healing and empowering, drawing strength from the very roots that once seemed to tether them to their familial pain.

Social support systems also play a critical role in the resilience of those dealing with inherited trauma. The presence of empathetic friends, family members, or even professional therapists can provide a reflective surface for one's experiences. In the presence of a compassionate other, an individual can begin to untangle the complex web of emotions and begin the process of understanding and integrating their trauma.

Mindfulness and meditation have also emerged as powerful tools for those grappling with the echoes of ancestral suffering. These practices encourage a presence of mind that can help to quiet the tumultuous inner dialogue that trauma can provoke. By fostering a sense of calm and centeredness, mindfulness can help individuals approach their inherited challenges with a clearer perspective, making it possible to respond rather than react to the emotional triggers they encounter.

Physical activity and connection to the body are equally important. Trauma can often lead to a disconnection from one's physical self. Still, activities such as yoga, dance, or even simple exercise can help to bridge that gap. By becoming attuned to the sensations and needs of their bodies, individuals can reclaim a sense of agency and vitality that trauma may have diminished.

It is important to note that coping mechanisms are not a one-size-fits-all solution. What offers profound relief to one person may not resonate with another. The key is the exploration and the willingness to engage with various strategies to discover what best facilitates one's journey toward healing.

Moreover, resilience should not be mistaken for a lack of vulnerability. It is not the absence of pain or struggle but rather the capacity to persevere despite it. Resilience is the courage to confront the darkest chapters of one's family history and seek the light that can lead to a more hopeful narrative for future generations.

In this ongoing process, individuals may find that their coping mechanisms evolve. As they grow and change, so do their needs and strategies for meeting them. This evolution is a natural part of the healing journey. It is a sign that the individual is not static but is instead moving forward, ever adapting to the contours of their inherited landscape.

The resilience of those who face inherited family trauma is a profound reminder of the human capacity for growth and transformation. It is a testament to the strength that can emerge when one faces the past with courage and the future with hope.

Chapter Summary

- Trauma has long-lasting psychological effects that can affect not just the individual but also their descendants, altering their mental health.
- Inherited trauma can lead to heightened anxiety and depression, presenting as a constant sense of unease or profound existential despair.
- Transmission of trauma can occur through behavioral modeling, biochemical changes due to stress, and epigenetic modifications that affect gene expression.
- Recognizing inherited trauma patterns is the first step toward healing, with therapy, mindfulness, and medication as potential aids.
- Inherited family trauma can predispose individuals to anxiety and depression, but understanding and therapeutic intervention can foster resilience and recovery.
- Cognitive echoes from inherited trauma can shape thought patterns and beliefs, influencing perceptions and reactions to the world.
- Dreams and imagination can vividly reflect inherited trauma, with recurring nightmares and themes that resonate with ancestral experiences.
- Coping mechanisms and resilience are vital to navigating inherited trauma, with creative expression, rituals, social support, mindfulness, and physical activity as helpful strategies.

4

THE LANGUAGE OF TRAUMA: COMMUNICATION AND EXPRESSION

Narratives of Pain: Storytelling and Memory

In the realm of inherited family trauma, the stories that are passed down from generation to generation carry with them not only the explicit narratives of our ancestors' experiences but also the implicit emotional residue of their pain. These narratives of pain, woven into the very fabric of family history, are often recounted through storytelling and the shared memory of the collective.

In this context, storytelling serves as a powerful vessel for transmitting trauma. It is a means by which experiences are given a voice, allowing for the externalization of internal suffering. Recounting one's story, or the stories of those before us, is not merely a recitation of facts; it is an emotional journey that can rekindle the smoldering embers of past anguish.

Memory plays a pivotal role in this process. It is selective, often highlighting the most traumatic events, and through this lens, the past is remembered and conveyed. The stories told are rarely neutral; they are colored by the emotions they evoke in the teller and the listener. Though personal, these memories become shared artifacts within the family, shaping future generations' identity and emotional landscape.

The power of these narratives lies not only in the words spoken but also in the silences between them. It is within these silences that the unspeakable is often housed. The things too painful to articulate, the experiences that words fail to capture, reside in the quiet moments that punctuate the storytelling. These silences speak volumes, conveying the depth of trauma that can be too overwhelming to express verbally.

As these stories are told and retold, they are not static; they evolve with each iteration, influenced by the narrator's current emotional state and understanding. How a story is told at one moment may differ from its recounting years later as insights are gained and perspectives shift. This fluidity allows for a dynamic engagement with the past, which can be healing and potentially retraumatizing.

The act of storytelling within the context of inherited family trauma is not merely about preserving history; it is about grappling with the emotional inheritance that accompanies that history. It is a process through which understanding can be sought and, perhaps, a measure of peace can be found. Through the narratives of pain, individuals and families engage in a complex dance with their past, attempting to find a way to integrate these stories into their lives without being consumed by them.

In the ongoing journey to comprehend and mitigate the effects of inherited trauma, it is essential to recognize the profound impact that storytelling and memory have on individuals and the collective family psyche. By giving voice to the pain of the past, there is hope for a future where the weight of this inheritance can be acknowledged, understood, and transformed with time and effort.

Nonverbal Transmission: Gestures, Posture, and Silence

Inherited family trauma often weaves itself into the fabric of our being, not only through the stories told but also through the silent language of our bodies. The way we carry ourselves, the gestures we make, and the silences we hold can be powerful communicators of the experiences that have shaped us, often without our conscious awareness.

Gestures, those subtle or pronounced movements we make with our hands, faces, or bodies, can be echoes of past traumas. A clenched fist, a furrowed brow, or a chronic avoidance of eye contact might be the physical manifestations of emotional pain passed down through generations. These gestures can become a part of a family's behavioral vocabulary, a nonverbal lexicon of shared suffering.

Posture, too, tells its own story. The way one might slump their shoulders, protectively hunch over, or hold tension in the neck can be indicative of internalized trauma. It's as if the body remembers what the mind tries to forget, and it expresses this memory in a language all its own. The body's posture can be a reservoir for anxiety, fear, and the weight of unspoken stories that have been inherited from those who came before.

Silence, in the context of inherited family trauma, is particularly poignant. It is not merely the absence of sound but a presence filled with unarticulated emotions and untold stories. It can be a heavy blanket under which the unspeakable is hidden or a protective space where healing begins. The silence of a family can be a powerful transmitter of trauma, as what is not said is often as influential as what is spoken aloud. It can be a learned response, a way of coping passed down, teaching each generation to internalize their pain and communicate through a quiet language of shared understanding.

The nonverbal cues we inherit and perpetuate within our families are not always negative. They can also be a source of strength and resilience. A gentle touch, a warm embrace, or a steady, supportive stance can be nonverbal affirmations of love and solidarity that have helped previous generations endure and can provide a foundation of support for the present.

Understanding the nonverbal transmission of inherited family trauma requires a keen sense of observation and a deep empathy for how these unspoken elements can influence our lives. Only by recognizing and acknowledging these silent communicators can we begin to address the trauma they represent and transform them into expressions of healing and growth. As we move forward, we find that the arts and creative expression offer a powerful avenue for this transformation, providing a voice to the voiceless gestures, postures, and silences that have shaped our existence.

Artistic and Creative Outlets

In the realm of inherited family trauma, where words often fall short, and silence can be deafening, individuals may find solace and expression through the universal language of art. Artistic and creative outlets serve as a conduit for the emotions and experiences that are otherwise inexpressible in the traditional lexicon of trauma discourse.

The canvas becomes a silent witness to the internal turmoil, the paintbrush a tool to navigate the labyrinth of generational pain. Through strokes and colors, the artist communicates the nuances of their inherited sorrow, often revealing insights previously obscured by the limitations of verbal language. Creating art is not merely a form of self-expression; it is a dialogue with the past, a way of understanding and integrating the experiences woven into the fabric of one's lineage.

Similarly, the written word, though paradoxically part of the language system, can transcend its boundaries through poetry and narrative. The rhythm and flow of poetry allow for an abstraction and distillation of emotions, capturing the essence of trauma in a personal and universal way. On the other hand, narrative writing can be a systematic excavation of family history, a way to give voice to the stories that have been silenced, and a means to reconstruct a fragmented identity.

Music, with its melodies and harmonies, resonates with the unspeakable elements of our shared human experience. It can evoke the deepest of emotions and memories, often serving as a bridge between the present and the past, between what is said and what is felt. Music can be a healing force for those with inherited trauma. This vibrational companion understands without judgment.

Dance and movement therapy offers another dimension of expression. The body, which often bears the bodily imprint of trauma, finds its language through movement, releasing the stories etched in muscle and sinew. Inherited patterns of tension and holding can be explored and, with time, transformed into movements of liberation and resilience.

These artistic and creative outlets offer a means of communication and a path to healing. They allow for a reclamation of agency, providing a space where one can safely explore and reshape the narrative of their inherited trauma. Through these practices, individuals can begin to untangle the threads of their family's past, weaving a new tapestry of understanding and meaning that honors their history while forging a new way forward.

In embracing the arts as a form of expression, we acknowledge the complexity of human emotion and how trauma can shape, but not define, our existence. In the act of creation, it is here that the language of trauma finds its most profound and eloquent voice.

The Role of Language in Shaping Experience

Language is not merely a tool for communication; it is the architecture of our inner world, the framework through which we construct reality and give shape to our experiences. In the realm of inherited family trauma, language becomes a vessel that carries the weight of past generations, often without our conscious awareness. Through language, unspoken pains are hinted at, and through language, the unspeakable is sometimes inadvertently revealed.

How families communicate about trauma—or choose to remain

silent—can significantly influence how individuals understand and internalize their ancestral past. The absence of language, the voids where stories should reside, can be as telling as the stories themselves. Silence can be a heavy burden, suggesting that some truths are too painful to articulate or that they must be cloistered away to protect the family's fabric. Yet, this silence can create an undercurrent of anxiety, a sense that there are obscured pieces of one's identity, fragments of a puzzle that one is not permitted to assemble.

Conversely, the presence of language can be equally potent. The words chosen to describe past traumas can color the emotional landscape of future generations. A family that speaks of its past with bitterness and resentment may inadvertently instill a sense of victimhood and anger in its descendants. On the other hand, narratives that emphasize resilience and survival can imbue a sense of strength and hope. The language used to convey these stories is not neutral; it is imbued with the power to shape perceptions, beliefs, and emotional responses.

Moreover, the metaphors and analogies employed to describe inherited trauma can either illuminate or obscure our understanding. When we use warlike metaphors, for example, we may adopt a combative stance towards our inherited pain, viewing it as an enemy to be defeated. Let's speak of trauma as a journey. We might instead see ourselves as travelers navigating a landscape that requires understanding and exploration. The choice of metaphor is not merely stylistic; it is a cognitive framing that can alter our approach to healing and self-awareness.

Language also plays a critical role in the intergenerational transmission of trauma. Research has shown that the narratives parents share with their children can either perpetuate a cycle of trauma or contribute to its resolution. When stories are shared with care and consciousness, acknowledging the pain while also encapsulating the lessons and growth that emerged from it, they can help the next generation contextualize and integrate these experiences into their lives healthily.

In essence, the role of language in shaping experience is profound. Through language, we encode and perpetuate our familial narratives. Through language, we have the opportunity to reframe and transform them. As we move forward, it becomes essential to consider how we can use language to convey inherited trauma and foster healing and growth. By cultivating new dialogues that honor the past while rewriting the trauma narrative, we can break the cycle and chart a course toward collective healing.

Breaking the Cycle: New Dialogues

In the intricate weave of human existence, the threads of trauma are often woven so intricately into the fabric of our family histories that they become almost indistinguishable from the patterns of daily life. The language we use to communicate our experiences, as explored in the preceding discussion, not only reflects but also reinforces the enduring impact of these traumas. Here, in the realm of expression, we find the potential to unravel these threads and weave a new narrative. This section delves into the transformative power of creating new dialogues to break the cycle of inherited family trauma.

The journey of healing is not embarked upon in silence. It requires the courage to speak and the strength to listen. New dialogues begin with acknowledging the past, not as a place of residence but as a point of reference. It is essential to recognize the patterns of communication that have perpetuated trauma, to understand the unspoken rules that have governed family interactions, and to bring them into the light of conscious discourse.

Breaking the cycle necessitates a language that moves beyond the confines of blame, shame, and guilt. It requires a lexicon of compassion, empathy, and understanding. Families must learn to articulate their pain without fearing judgment or retribution. This involves cultivating a space where vulnerability is not equated with weakness, but rather seen as a profound act of bravery. In this space, individuals are encouraged to express their emotions, share their stories, and articulate their needs.

One of the most significant shifts in dialogue comes from the transition from passive to active language. Rather than speaking about trauma as something that merely happens to an individual or family, it is empowering to discuss the active steps being taken to heal and grow. This shift in language reflects a shift in agency, from being victims of circumstance to being architects of one's healing journey.

Moreover, new dialogues involve the interweaving of multiple perspectives. Inherited family trauma is not a monolith; it affects each member differently. Creating a multifaceted conversation that honors each person's unique experiences is crucial. This means actively listening to one another, asking open-ended questions, and resisting the urge to impose one's narrative onto someone else's experience.

It is also essential to integrate new forms of communication that may have yet to be present. For some, this may mean exploring non-verbal forms of expression such as art, music, or movement, which can serve as powerful conduits for emotions that words cannot capture. For others, it may involve learning to set boundaries and assertively communicate one's limits, a skill often eroded in environments where trauma has dictated interactions.

In breaking the cycle of inherited family trauma, we are not merely altering the way we speak; we are transforming the way we connect with ourselves. This transformation is not instantaneous. It is a process that unfolds through consistent effort, patience, and a willingness to embrace the discomfort of change. Each new dialogue is a step towards a future where the legacy of trauma is not one of pain and silence but one of healing and growth.

As we continue to explore the language of trauma and its expression, it becomes evident that the power to redefine our experiences lies within our grasp. Through new dialogues, we can begin to untangle the knots of the past and weave a narrative that supports resilience, fosters understanding, and celebrates the possibility of renewal.

Chapter Summary

- Family trauma is passed down through stories that carry emotional pain, affecting future generations.
- Storytelling allows for the externalization of internal suffering and can rekindle past anguish.

- Memory selectively highlights traumatic events, shaping identity and emotional responses within families.
- The unspeakable aspects of trauma often reside in the silences between stories, conveying the depth of pain.
- Stories evolve, influenced by the narrator's emotions and understanding, which can be healing or retraumatizing.
- Storytelling is a way to grapple with emotional inheritance and seek understanding and peace.
- Recognizing the impact of storytelling and memory is crucial in comprehending and mitigating inherited trauma.
- Artistic and creative outlets provide a means to express and heal from trauma that words cannot fully capture.

5

THE TIES THAT BIND: FAMILY DYNAMICS

Roles and Expectations within the Family System

Within family dynamics, each member often finds themselves cast in roles that are as defining as they are limiting. These roles, shaped by the expectations of the family unit, can be both a source of comfort and a catalyst for perpetuating inherited trauma. As we delve into the nuances of these roles and expectations, we must consider how they contribute to the complex tapestry of intergenerational narratives.

Roles within the family are frequently assigned early in life, often without conscious intent. The eldest child may become the 'responsible one,' shouldering burdens that exceed their years. At the same time, the youngest might be labeled the 'baby,' perpetually seen as needing protection. While seemingly benign, these roles can set the stage for a lifetime of scripted behavior that stifles individual growth and perpetuates familial patterns.

Expectations, too, are woven into the fabric of family life. They can be explicit, such as the anticipation that children will follow in their parent's footsteps, or implicit, like the unspoken belief that one must never show weakness or vulnerability. These expectations often arise from the family's collective experiences and traumas, handed down like heirlooms, sometimes treasured, other times borne out of obligation.

These roles and expectations can be heavy, mainly when they are at odds with a person's authentic self. A child who yearns for artistic expression may be constrained by the expectation to pursue a more 'practical' profession. Another might struggle with the role of peacemaker, suppressing their needs to maintain fragile family harmony. In such ways, the family system, while providing a sense of identity and belonging, can also inadvertently trap members in cycles of trauma and unfulfillment.

By recognizing these roles and expectations, individuals can begin to understand the origins of their pain and those who came before them—acknowledging that these roles are not fixed but rather malleable narratives that allow for the possibility of change. By challenging and reshaping these expectations, family members can start to heal from inherited trauma, crafting new roles that align with their true selves and fostering a family dynamic that supports individuality and growth.

As we transition from exploring roles and expectations, we must consider the concepts of enmeshment and differentiation. These psychological constructs further illuminate how family members can become entangled in each other's lives, sometimes to the detriment of their individual development. Understanding the delicate balance between closeness and autonomy within the family system is crucial in addressing the complex interplay of inherited family trauma.

Enmeshment and Differentiation

When discussing family dynamics, the concepts of enmeshment and differentiation stand out as pivotal elements that shape the relational patterns and, consequently, the transmission of trauma from one generation to the next. These two forces act as the yin and yang within family systems, each holding the potential to foster healthy relationships or perpetuate cycles of inherited trauma.

Enmeshment, a term that may evoke the image of threads too tightly woven together, refers to relationships where personal boundaries are diffused, individuality is diminished, and emotional autonomy is scarce. In an enmeshed family, members may feel a heightened responsibility for each other's emotional states and decisions, often leading to a loss of personal identity. The intentions behind such closeness can be rooted in love and the desire for unity. Still, when taken to the extreme, it can create an environment where the individual's emotional well-being is inextricably tied to the family's collective psyche.

This lack of boundaries can mean that trauma is not an isolated experience; instead, it becomes a shared burden, passed down through the generations as quickly as heirlooms or genetic traits. When one member of the family experiences trauma, the emotional fallout can ripple through the enmeshed network, leaving each person to carry a piece of the pain, often without the tools or understanding to process it independently.

Differentiation, on the other hand, offers a contrasting approach to family relationships. It is the process by which individuals within the family system develop a strong sense of self while remaining connected to their loved ones. Differentiation allows members to express their thoughts, feelings, and desires without fear of losing emotional support or family ties. It is the balance between autonomy and intimacy, where family members can support one another without sacrificing individuality.

In a differentiated family, trauma may still occur. Still, its legacy is less likely to be woven into the fabric of the family's collective identity. Members are better equipped to offer support without becoming entangled in the trauma. They can acknowledge the pain of the past and work towards healing without allowing it to define them or their relationships.

The journey from enmeshment to differentiation is a complex one. It requires a conscious effort to establish healthy boundaries and a willingness to confront and understand the trauma that has been inherited. It is a delicate dance between honoring the interconnectedness of the family and nurturing the individual's right to a separate, autonomous existence.

As we explore family dynamics, it is essential to recognize the role that scapegoating can play within these relational patterns. Often, when the balance between enmeshment and differentiation is lost, families may unconsciously assign the role of the scapegoat to one member, who then becomes the depository for the family's unresolved issues and trauma. Understanding this dynamic is crucial in unraveling the complex tapestry of inherited family trauma and in paving the way for healing and transformation.

Scapegoating and the Family Scapegoat

Within the complex network of family relationships, a role is as enduring as it is damaging—the family scapegoat. Often unwittingly appointed, this individual bears the brunt of the family's collective dysfunction, carrying the weight of blame for problems far beyond their control. The scapegoating process is not just a matter of assigning fault in times of conflict; it is a complex mechanism that can perpetuate inherited family trauma across generations.

To understand the phenomenon of scapegoating, one must first recognize its roots in the family's unconscious effort to manage pain and disavow internal conflict. When a family system is unable to confront and process its traumas—be they rooted in abuse, neglect, addiction, or other forms of emotional turmoil—it may unconsciously designate one member to symbolize these unresolved issues. This person becomes the repository for the family's unspoken grief, anger, and shame.

The role of the scapegoat is often solidified in childhood and can be alarmingly stable over time. A child who exhibits vulnerability or reacts strongly to the family's dysfunction may be more likely to be cast in this role. Once established, the scapegoat becomes the focal point for criticism, with their actions and behaviors subjected to disproportionate scrutiny. This dynamic can severely impact the individual's self-esteem, relationships, and overall mental health.

The scapegoat's journey is one of profound isolation. They are frequently misunderstood and marginalized, not only within the family but also in their interactions with the world at large. The internalized belief that they are inherently flawed or responsible for the family's distress can lead to a self-fulfilling prophecy, where the scapegoat struggles with personal and professional relationships, reinforcing the family's narrative.

Yet, the role of the scapegoat is not without its paradoxes. While they are burdened with blame, they are also often the member who is most aware of the family's toxic patterns. Their unique position can grant them the insight and motivation to seek change for themselves and their family. It is not uncommon for the scapegoat to be the first to seek therapy or to break the cycle of trauma by refusing to participate in the dysfunctional family script.

The healing process for a family scapegoat involves a deep and often painful reevaluation of their place within the family narrative. It requires dismantling long-held beliefs and recreating a self-identity eroded by years of misplaced blame. Through therapeutic interventions, support systems, and personal resilience, the scapegoat can begin to shed the burdens that were never theirs to carry and forge a path toward a healthier, autonomous life.

The journey of the scapegoat is symbolic of the broader struggles within a family grappling with inherited trauma. It is a role that illuminates how pain, if left unaddressed, can warp the bonds meant to offer support and love. In recognizing the dynamics of scapegoating, families can begin to untangle the threads of their shared history, confront the traumas that bind them, and move toward a future where each member is seen, heard, and valued for who they are.

Secrets, Lies, and Family Myths

Within the complex interplay of family interactions, secrets, and lies often serve as the silent architects of dysfunction, shaping the emotional landscape of generations. Like specters in the family narrative, these hidden truths cast long shadows over descendants' lives, often without their conscious awareness. The myths that families construct around these secrets become the bedrock of inherited trauma, a legacy passed down as indeed as genetic traits.

The power of secrets lies not only in the content of what is hidden but also in the act of concealment itself. When a family chooses to bury the truth, it inadvertently creates an environment where reality is malleable, and trust becomes a casualty. Children raised in such families may develop a keen sense of vigilance, an unconscious radar for the unspoken or the unseen. They learn to read between the lines, to listen for the silences that speak volumes. This hypervigilance, while adaptive in the context of uncertainty, can become a burden, a predisposition to anxiety that haunts relationships and personal development.

Lies, whether by omission or commission, weave a complex tapestry of alternate reality. Family members may play roles in a story that feels inauthentic, a narrative that doesn't align with their inner experience. The dissonance between the outward family myth and the internal sense of truth can lead to a profound sense of dislocation, a feeling of not belonging to the story of one's lineage.

The myths families create to justify or mask their secrets are often rooted in a desire to protect. Yet, this protection comes at a cost. The myth of the perfect family, the untarnished legacy, or the infallible parent can place an immense burden on the shoulders of those who know, deep down, that the reality is far more complex. The pressure to maintain the facade can lead to a pervasive sense of isolation as individuals struggle with the dichotomy of public image and private truth.

Moreover, the energy expended in maintaining these myths can detract from the family's ability to form genuine connections. Relationships may become transactional, based on the currency of shared delusion rather than authentic emotional exchange. The fear of what might happen if the truth were to emerge can lead to a fortress mentality, where the family unit becomes insular, and outsiders are viewed with suspicion.

The consequences of these dynamics are not confined to the emotional realm. The stress of living with secrets and lies can manifest in physical ailments, a phenomenon increasingly recognized by research into psychosomatic medicine. The body keeps its ledger of the heart's unspoken burdens.

As we consider the role of secrets, lies, and family myths in the context of inherited family trauma, it becomes clear that the path to healing is paved with truth. Unraveling the tapestries of deception requires courage and a willingness to face the discomfort of revelation. Yet, through this process of uncovering and understanding the hidden narratives of our past, we can begin to free ourselves from their grip. In the light of truth, the chains of inherited trauma may begin to loosen, allowing future generations to write their own stories unencumbered by the weight of unspoken history.

The Impact of Loss and Grief

In the labyrinth of family dynamics, the echoes of loss and grief are perhaps the most profound and enduring. They are the silent currents that shape the emotional landscape of generations, carving deep channels into the collective memory of a lineage. The way a family navigates the treacherous waters of grief can leave indelible marks on its members, marks that may be passed down as inherited trauma.

When a family experiences a loss, the immediate reaction is often an outpouring of grief. This is the visible part of the iceberg, which can be acknowledged, shared, and, to some extent, socially sanctioned. However, beneath the surface lies a complex web of emotions and responses that may not find expression in tears or words. It is in this submerged silence that the seeds of inherited trauma can take root.

The bereavement process is not a linear journey with a clear endpoint. It is a cyclical and often unpredictable passage through various stages of denial, anger, bargaining, depression, and acceptance, as famously outlined by Elisabeth Kübler-Ross. Yet, not every individual or family moves through these stages in a textbook fashion. Some may become trapped in one stage, unable to advance toward healing. Others may oscillate between stages or even experience them simultaneously. This can create a family environment where grief is a constant, albeit sometimes unspoken, presence.

The impact of unresolved grief is particularly potent. When the pain of loss is not processed, it can become a silent specter at the family table, influencing interactions, decisions, and even the family's narrative about itself. Children, even those born after the loss, can inherit this unresolved grief, internalizing the sorrow and confusion they sense in their elders. They may grow up feeling something amiss, a vague melancholy they cannot quite name or understand.

Moreover, the way a family communicates about loss—or fails to communicate—can significantly shape the grief experience. In families where open expression of emotions is discouraged or where grief is considered a private matter, children may learn to suppress their feelings. This emotional stoicism can be mistaken for resilience. Still, it may be a form of avoidance that hampers grief processing. The unspoken rule that 'we do not talk about our pain' can lead to a legacy of emotional isolation and difficulty in forming deep, authentic connections.

Conversely, in families where grief is expressed excessively or dysfunctionally, children may learn to equate love with suffering. They might believe that to be a part of the family, one must carry a portion of the collective pain. This can lead to a pattern of martyrdom or co-dependency, where individuals sacrifice their well-being in the service of the family's unresolved grief.

The rituals and traditions a family adopts in the wake of loss can also play a role in the transmission of trauma. Some families may create meaningful ceremonies that honor the deceased and provide a sense of closure. Others may cling to rituals that, while intended to keep the memory of the loved one alive, inadvertently anchor the family to the moment of loss, preventing them from moving forward.

It is essential to recognize that inherited family trauma is not a destiny set in stone. With awareness and support, families can interrupt the cycle of transmitted grief. This may involve seeking therapy, fostering open communication, and creating new narratives that acknowledge the past while embracing the future. Healing inherited trauma is akin to tending to a garden that has been neglected; it requires patience, care, and the willingness to confront the weeds that choke growth. As families learn to process their grief, they can cultivate resilience and hope, ensuring that the ties that bind them are woven with love and understanding, rather than sorrow and regret.

Chapter Summary

- Family roles and expectations can be limiting and contribute to intergenerational trauma.
- Roles like the 'responsible eldest' or 'protected youngest' can stifle individual growth and perpetuate family patterns.
- Expectations may be explicit or implicit, often stemming from collective family experiences and traumas.
- These roles and expectations can trap family members in cycles of trauma and unfulfillment.
- Recognizing and challenging these roles can lead to healing and creating new, supportive family dynamics.
- Family enrichment can lead to diffused boundaries and shared trauma, while differentiation allows for individuality within family connections.
- Scapegoating within families assigns one member to bear the dysfunction, leading to isolation and potential insight for change.
- Family secrets and myths can create dysfunction and inherited trauma, with healing coming from uncovering and confronting these hidden narratives.

6

SOCIETAL REFLECTIONS: THE CULTURAL CONTEXT

Cultural Trauma and Collective Memory

Within the fabric of human life, the threads of cultural trauma and collective memory are inextricably woven together, creating patterns that tell the stories of communities and nations. These patterns, rich with the hues of shared pain and resilience, do not fade with generations; instead, they are inherited, subtly influencing the fabric of family life and individual identity.

Cultural trauma refers to a profound disruption that affects a collective. It is a wound inflicted upon the social consciousness of a community, reverberating through generations in the form of shared memories, behaviors, and values. This trauma can arise from events such as war, genocide, colonization, or natural disasters. The repercussions are not limited to those who directly experienced the event; they ripple outward, affecting those who inherit the legacy of the past.

Collective memory is the shared pool of knowledge and information in a community that extends beyond individual experiences. It encompasses the narratives that a culture preserves and passes down, shaping the identity and consciousness of its members. These memories are not static but actively maintained, constructed, and reconstructed through cultural practices such as storytelling, rituals, and education.

The interplay between cultural trauma and collective memory is complex. On the one hand, collective memory serves as a repository for the communal understanding of trauma, ensuring that the experiences of the past are not forgotten. On the other hand, it can also act as a framework through which current experiences are interpreted, potentially perpetuating the cycle of trauma.

Inherited family trauma, then, is the personal echo of these more significant cultural phenomena. It is how these historical and collective experiences shape the psychological and emotional landscape of individuals within a family. The way a family discusses (or remains silent about) past hardships, the emotional climate surrounding these narratives, and the behaviors and coping mechanisms developed in response all stem from the broader cultural context of trauma and memory.

Families may carry the weight of cultural trauma in their collective psyche, often without a conscious understanding of its origins. The stories of ancestors who survived or succumbed to great adversities are not merely tales of the past; they are the undercurrents that can influence family dynamics, parenting styles, and individual mental health. The traumas their forebears endured can shape how parents express affection, handle conflict, and deal with stress. In turn, these patterns can be passed down to their children.

The recognition of these inherited patterns is crucial for healing and growth. It allows individuals and families to contextualize their experiences within their culture's larger narrative, understand that their personal struggles may be part of a collective struggle, and find solidarity and support within their community. It also opens the door to breaking cycles of trauma by fostering awareness, empathy, and the development of new, healthier behavior patterns.

As we delve deeper into the influence of social norms and values on inherited family trauma, it becomes clear that the cultural context is both a source of wounds and a potential pathway to healing. The values a society upholds, the norms it enforces, and how it addresses—or fails to address—its collective traumas all play a role in shaping the experiences of individuals and families. Understanding this intricate relationship is essential for anyone seeking to comprehend the full scope of inherited family trauma and to contribute to the collective journey toward healing and resilience.

The Influence of Social Norms and Values

Within the complex weave of human society, the warp and weft of social norms and values shape the fabric of our daily interactions and influence how inherited family trauma is perceived, processed, and perpetuated. As we delve deeper into the cultural context of such trauma, it becomes increasingly evident that the collective ethos of a community can either exacerbate the silent suffering passed down through generations or provide a nurturing ground for healing and transformation.

Social norms, the unwritten rules that govern behavior in groups and societies, often dictate the response to trauma. In some cultures, stoicism and resilience are highly valued, and individuals are expected to bear their burdens silently without outwardly acknowledging their pain. This cultural expectation can lead to a suppression of traumatic experiences, as individuals may feel compelled to maintain a facade of strength and normalcy. The internalization of trauma, in this context, becomes a hidden legacy, one that is silently inherited by offspring who may sense the unspoken anguish of their forebears but lack the vocabulary or permission to address it.

Conversely, open communication and emotional expression can foster an environment where discussing past hurts is not only allowed but encouraged. In such societies, the acknowledgment of trauma is seen as a step towards healing, and sharing one's story is viewed as an act of courage rather than a sign of weakness. This cultural milieu can mitigate the transmission of trauma by creating spaces for dialogue, reflection, and collective support.

The influence of social norms and values extends to the institutions that uphold them. Educational systems, religious organizations, and the media all play pivotal roles in either reinforcing the silence surrounding inherited trauma or challenging the status quo. Educational curricula that study historical traumas and their impact on present generations can enlighten young minds about the complexities of inherited pain. Religious and spiritual practices that offer rituals for mourning and forgiveness can provide solace and a path to release the burdens of the past. Meanwhile, media representation that humanizes the experiences of those carrying the weight of ancestral trauma can shift public perception and foster empathy.

However, this cultural scaffolding has its challenges. Norms and values are not static; they evolve with time and can be subject to the whims of those in power. What is considered taboo today may be openly discussed tomorrow, and vice versa. This fluidity can leave individuals grappling with inherited trauma in a liminal space, uncertain of whether their experiences will be met with understanding or judgment.

Moreover, the intersectionality of identity—race, gender, class, and more—complicates the landscape of inherited trauma. Marginalized groups may face additional barriers in seeking recognition and healing for their inherited wounds, as societal prejudices can silence their narratives or minimize their pain. The interplay of these identities with cultural norms and values can either compound the trauma or catalyze a collective movement toward healing.

As we consider the influence of social norms and values on inherited family trauma, it is crucial to recognize the power of cultural change. By challenging harmful norms and advocating for values that promote healing and understanding, societies can begin to address the deep-seated traumas passed down through generations. Through this cultural evolution, we can hope to see a future where the legacy of trauma is not one of silent suffering but of resilience and renewal.

Immigration, Displacement, and Diaspora

Within the mosaic of human existence, the threads of immigration, displacement, and diaspora are interwoven with complex patterns of inherited family trauma. These phenomena, often driven by necessity, ambition, or survival, carry the weight of cultural upheaval and the silent echoes of ancestral struggles. As families traverse borders and oceans, they do not merely transport belongings; they carry the intangible legacy of their forebears, a legacy that often includes the trauma of leaving behind everything familiar.

The act of immigration is a disruption of the narrative continuity of a family's history. This decision can be both empowering and disorienting, as it promises new beginnings while severing ties with the past. The immigrant journey is fraught with challenges, from the physical dangers of the journey to the psychological toll of adjusting to a new society. The displacement accompanying immigration can lead to a sense of rootless-ness, a feeling of being suspended between two worlds, neither entirely belonging to the old nor entirely accepted by the new.

For children of immigrants, this sense of displacement is inherited, often without the accompanying memories of the homeland. They are born into a diaspora, a scattered community whose shared history is marked by the collective trauma of dislocation. These children may grapple with a fragmented identity, piecing together their sense of self from stories, traditions, and the lingering effects of their parent's experiences. The trauma of immigration does not dissipate with the crossing of a border; it lingers, manifesting in the emotional and cultural dissonance that can permeate a family for generations.

The cultural context of the new society plays a pivotal role in shaping the immigrant experience. Acceptance, integration, and the opportunity to thrive are not guaranteed. Instead, immigrants often encounter barriers that hinder their ability to participate fully in their new home's social fabric. Language barriers, economic disparities, and cultural misunderstandings can exacerbate the sense of otherness, reinforcing the trauma of displacement.

Moreover, the diaspora community can serve as both a sanctuary and a source of tension. Within it is a collective memory of the homeland and a shared understanding of the immigrant experience. Yet, there can also be pressure to conform to the expectations of the diaspora to maintain cultural purity in a constantly changing land. This pressure can create a rift between generations as younger members navigate the delicate balance of honoring their heritage while seeking to belong in a society that may view them with suspicion or indifference.

The inherited trauma of immigration, displacement, and diaspora is thus a complex interplay of loss, adaptation, and resilience. It is a narrative that unfolds over lifetimes, with each generation adding its chapter to the family story. As we delve deeper into the societal implications of these experiences, we must also consider how racism, discrimination, and the intergenerational impact of these prejudices further shape the lives of those who have left their homelands in search of a better future.

Racism, Discrimination, and Intergenerational Impact

Throughout our existence, the threads of racism and discrimination are woven with particular darkness, their shadows stretching across generations, imprinting a legacy of pain and resilience in the fabric of family narratives. The intergenerational impact of these societal scourges is profound, often manifesting in ways that are subtle yet deeply entrenched within the psyche of those who bear the weight of historical injustices.

The concept of inherited family trauma is not merely an abstract psychological theory; it is a palpable reality for many. The silent whisper of anxiety lingers in the hearts of parents as they prepare their children for the prejudices they may face. It is the internalized oppression that stifles ambition and the unspoken grief that accompanies the stories of ancestors who endured unimaginable hardships simply because of their race or ethnicity.

For communities that have been marginalized, the trauma does not begin and end with a single event or generation. It is perpetuated through systemic inequalities, microaggressions in daily interactions, and the collective memory of historical atrocities that are too often sanitized or erased from the dominant cultural narrative. The psychological armor developed as a defense mechanism against these assaults does not quickly shed; it becomes part of the inheritance passed down, a complex interplay of resilience and vulnerability.

This inherited trauma can manifest in various forms, from the heightened vigilance that comes with the knowledge of one's skin color being a potential threat to others to the deep-seated fear of authority figures whose roles have historically been to oppress rather than to protect. It can lead to a profound sense of dislocation, even in one's homeland, and the internalization of negative stereotypes that erode self-esteem and foster a sense of otherness.

Yet, within this landscape of pain, there is also the potential for profound strength and solidarity. Families and communities share not only the burden of their collective trauma but also the wisdom and coping strategies that have allowed them to survive and, in many cases, to thrive despite the odds. The stories of resistance and triumph are as much a part of the legacy as the stories of suffering.

Understanding the intergenerational impact of racism and discrimination is crucial in the journey towards healing. It requires an acknowledgment of the past, an awareness of the present, and a commitment to a future where such legacies no longer dictate the boundaries of one's life. It calls for a compassionate and informed approach to addressing the wounds that, though invisible to the eye, are etched deeply into the hearts and minds of those affected.

As we move towards a cultural context in which healing is possible and actively pursued, we must recognize the resilience cultivated through generations of adversity. The path to healing is not linear or uniform. Still, it is paved with the collective efforts of individuals and communities who seek to transform the pain of the past into a foundation for a more just and empathetic world.

Healing in a Cultural Context

Within the complex fabric of human existence, the threads of trauma, particularly those inherited from our forebears, are woven with a resilience that is as commendable as it is complex. As we delve into healing within a cultural context, we must recognize that the path to recovery is not merely an individual journey. Still, it is deeply embedded within the cultural fabric that clothes our collective identity.

Culture, in its vast and varied forms, provides a backdrop against which the narrative of trauma and healing unfolds. Within this cultural framework, individuals find the symbols, rituals, and collective stories that can hinder or facilitate the healing process. To understand healing in a cultural context, we must first acknowledge that the very definition of trauma and the strategies for coping with it are culturally contingent.

The cultural context offers a repository of healing practices honed over generations. These practices, from traditional ceremonies and rites to storytelling and communal gatherings, serve as a conduit for expressing and processing the pain often buried within the collective psyche. They allow for the sharing of burdens, the validation of experiences, and the re-establishment of a sense of belonging and identity that trauma can disrupt.

Moreover, the role of the community must be balanced in the healing process. In many cultures, the community acts as a mirror reflecting the individual's pain, thus acknowledging its existence and legitimizing the individual's experience. This communal recognition is the first step towards healing, as it breaks the isolation that trauma can impose. The community then becomes a source of support, offering a network of relationships that can provide practical assistance, emotional comfort, and a path back to social engagement.

However, the cultural context can also present unique challenges to healing. Cultural stigmas attached to mental health, a legacy of silence surrounding trauma, or a collective identity that may prioritize endurance over the expression of suffering can all act as barriers. In such environments, seeking help may be seen as a deviation from the norm, and those who do so may face misunderstanding or ostracization.

Navigating these cultural complexities is crucial to fostering cultural competence among those who provide support and therapy. Understanding the cultural narratives and values that shape an individual's worldview can guide the healing process in a direction that resonates with their identity and experiences. Therapists and healers must recognize and incorporate cultural strengths into their practices, whether through language, metaphor, or culturally specific therapeutic interventions.

In the broader societal context, there is a growing recognition of the need for culturally sensitive approaches to healing. This includes acknowledging historical injustices and their ongoing impact on communities and ensuring that institutional support systems are attuned to the cultural dimensions of trauma. Policies and programs designed to address inherited family trauma must be crafted with an awareness of the cultural narratives that underpin the communities they aim to serve.

Therefore, healing in a cultural context is an intricate dance between honoring the wisdom of traditional healing practices and integrating the insights of contemporary therapeutic approaches. It is about creating spaces where individuals can find their voice within the chorus of their community and where the echoes of past traumas can be transformed into narratives of resilience and hope. As we continue to explore the multifaceted nature of inherited family trauma, it is this cultural lens that allows us to see the full spectrum of the human capacity for healing and growth.

Chapter Summary

- Cultural trauma refers to a profound disruption in a community, affecting collective memory and identity across generations.

- Collective memory is the shared knowledge within a community that shapes its members' identity and is actively maintained through cultural practices.
- The interplay between cultural trauma and collective memory can perpetuate trauma cycles or serve as a repository for communal understanding.
- Inherited family trauma is how historical and collective experiences shape individuals' psychological and emotional landscapes within a family.
- The traumas endured by ancestors can influence family dynamics, parenting styles, and individual mental health.
- Recognizing inherited patterns is critical to healing, allowing individuals to contextualize their struggles within a larger collective narrative.
- Social norms and values influence how inherited family trauma is perceived and processed, either reinforcing silence or fostering healing environments.
- Immigration, displacement, and diaspora introduce complex patterns of inherited trauma, including cultural upheaval and identity fragmentation.

7

THE JOURNEY WITHIN: PERSONAL STORIES

Voices from the Shadows: Personal Narratives

In the quiet recesses of our minds, where the echoes of our ancestors' experiences still resonate, we find the personal narratives that shape our understanding of inherited family trauma. These are the voices from the shadows, the stories that often go untold yet hold the power to influence generations.

One such narrative belongs to Maria, whose grandfather survived a war that ravaged his homeland and psyche. Though he never spoke of the horrors he witnessed, the silent ripples of his pain lapped through the family lineage. Maria grew up in a household where the air was thick with unspoken grief, a grief that she could taste but not name. It was only in her thirties, when she began to unravel her anxiety and inexplicable fears that she traced their roots to the grandfather she had never met. His trauma, unaddressed and unacknowledged, had become a silent heirloom.

Then there's David, whose mother endured a tumultuous and abusive marriage. David learned to walk on eggshells, internalizing the volatility of his childhood home. As an adult, he found himself inexplicably drawn to partners who mirrored the chaos he had known as a child. It was a pattern etched into his being, a learned response to a trauma that predated his memories. It was only through recognizing this pattern that he began seeking a different path that led away from the shadows of inherited pain.

These stories, and countless others like them, reveal the intricate web of our familial tapestries. Each thread is a story, a memory, a piece of a larger picture we carry. The weight of these inherited narratives can be heavy, and the journey to understanding and healing is often solitary. Yet, it is within the sharing of these personal narratives that we find a collective solace. When we give voice to the shadows, we illuminate the paths that our ancestors could not find, and in doing so, we forge new trails for ourselves and the generations to come.

Storytelling is not merely a recounting of events but an act of liberation. We acknowledge the depth of our shared human experience by bringing these personal narratives into the light. We validate not only our pain but also the pain of those who came before us. This acknowledgment is the first step toward healing, a step that many find themselves taking within the pages of their own lives long before they ever seek the guidance of therapists or the solace of support groups.

As we turn the page from the voices that have long been relegated to the shadows, we prepare to explore the transformative power of acknowledgment and validation. It is here that we will delve into the profound impact that recognition and acceptance can have on the journey toward healing inherited family trauma.

The Power of Acknowledgment and Validation

In the weave of human existence, the threads of our ancestors' hardships are often interwoven with our own, creating patterns that can either confine or guide us. As we delve into the personal stories of those who carry inherited family trauma, we uncover a profound truth: the act of acknowledging and validating these inherited pains is not merely a step toward healing—it is a transformative power in its own right.

For many, the journey within begins with a whisper—a sense that the emotions and reactions they experience are not solely their own. It's a realization that the anxiety felt before a family gathering or the inexplicable sadness that clouds a seemingly happy occasion may echo past generations' unresolved grief and suffering. These whispers grow louder, demanding attention, and the courageous act of listening takes the first steps toward acknowledgment.

Acknowledgment is a declaration that the trauma endured by previous generations matters. It is a conscious effort to shine a light on the dark corners of a family's history, to say, "This happened, and it affected us." It validates the pain that has silently shaped lives and relationships. In acknowledging inherited trauma, individuals permit themselves to explore the depth of their emotional inheritance without judgment or dismissal.

Validation follows acknowledgment like a balm. It is the empathetic response that says, "Your feelings are real, and they are worthy of attention." It is the external confirmation from loved ones, therapists, or support groups that the struggle one faces is legitimate and understood. Validation provides a mirror in which the true impact of inherited trauma is reflected, allowing those affected to see themselves and their experiences clearly, perhaps for the first time.

The power of acknowledgment and validation lies in their ability to break the cycle of silence that often surrounds inherited trauma. They create a space where stories can be shared without fear of stigma or disbelief. In this space, individuals find that their narratives are not isolated incidents but part of a more extensive, communal history. This realization fosters a sense of belonging and connection, vital for healing.

Moreover, acknowledgment and validation are not passive acts but dynamic processes that engage the intellect and emotions. They require an ongoing commitment to self-awareness and compassion for oneself and the generations that came before. Through these processes, individuals differentiate which parts of their emotional landscape are genuinely theirs and which are inherited. This differentiation is crucial for developing a sense of autonomy and making conscious choices about which legacies to carry forward and which to release.

As we journey with those who have embarked on this path of acknowledgment and validation, we witness the emergence of resilience and strength. Facing inherited trauma with honesty and compassion becomes a powerful testament to the human spirit's capacity for growth and transformation. It is a reminder that while we may inherit the traumas of our forebears, we also inherit their courage and ability to overcome.

In the next breaths of our exploration, we will gaze toward the turning points and catalysts that propel individuals from acknowledgment to action, from understanding to change. These moments mark the beginning of a new legacy that honors the past while forging a healthier, more conscious future.

Turning Points and Catalysts for Change

In life, each thread represents a story, a lineage, and a history passed down through generations. The colors may fade or change, but the fabric remains connected, often carrying the subtle yet profound imprints of inherited family trauma. As we delve into the personal narratives that make up the journey within, we encounter individuals at the precipice of transformation—moments that serve as turning points and catalysts for change.

These stories are not mere anecdotes; they are the living, breathing experiences of people who have faced the daunting task of confronting the silent legacies that have shaped their existence. The turning points are as diverse as the individuals themselves. Yet, they share a common thread: the realization that the cycles of the past need not dictate the patterns of the future.

For some, the catalyst for change is a singular, life-altering event—a birth, a death, a confrontation with mortality that brings the hidden traumas of the past to the surface. For others, it is a slow awakening, a series of subtle cues that accumulate over time, leading to the undeniable truth that their pain is not entirely their own.

One such story is that of Elena, a third-generation immigrant whose grandparents fled war-torn Europe. The resilience they needed to rebuild their lives in a new country was a source of pride in her family. Yet, beneath the surface of that resilience was an undercurrent of unspoken anxiety and hyper-vigilance that permeated Elena's upbringing. It wasn't until Elena faced her battle with anxiety that she began to unravel the threads of inherited trauma, recognizing the patterns that had been invisibly woven into her behavior.

Another narrative unfolds with Michael, whose father's unexplained outbursts of anger and subsequent withdrawal into silence were the backdrop of his childhood. It was only upon becoming a father himself that Michael felt the weight of unprocessed grief—grief that he later discovered was rooted in his father's experience as a child of an alcoholic parent. The birth of his daughter was the turning point. This catalyst propelled him to seek help and break the cycle of emotional suppression that had been handed down to him.

While deeply personal, these turning points are also universal in their resonance. They are the moments when the past is held up to the light, examined, and understood not as a determinant of fate but as a map that has guided one to the present. With this understanding comes the possibility of charting a new course that honors the journey of those who came before while forging a path toward healing.

The courage to confront inherited family trauma is not a solitary endeavor. It is a collective journey that requires empathy, support, and the shared wisdom of those who have walked similar paths. As we witness these stories of transformation, we are reminded that the legacy of the past need not be a burden. Instead, it can be the catalyst that inspires us to heal, grow, and redefine the narrative for future generations.

In this journey within, the turning points and catalysts for change are not just markers of individual growth; they are beacons of hope for all who seek to understand the intricate web of inherited trauma. They are a testament to the human spirit's capacity to transcend the confines of history and embrace the potential for renewal.

Legacy Bearers: The Weight of History

Within our human experience, the threads of our ancestors' hardships are often interwoven with our own, creating patterns that may go unnoticed until we take a closer look. As we delve into the personal stories of those who carry the weight of history, we find that the legacy of inherited family trauma is not just a relic of the past but a living, breathing presence in the lives of descendants.

Consider Sarah, whose grandfather survived a brutal war. The horrors he witnessed were etched into the silence that filled their home. Sarah grew up in the shadow of unspoken grief, a quiet understanding that some things were too painful to voice. It was only when she found herself grappling with inexplicable anxiety that the connection to her grandfather's unhealed wounds became clear. Her journey to address her struggles led her to uncover the buried stories of her family's past, revealing the unseen influence of inherited trauma.

Then there's Adam, whose family history was riddled with addiction. The cycle seemed unbreakable, each generation succumbing to the same destructive patterns. It was as if the addiction was part of the family legacy, passed down like a dark heirloom. But Adam's story took a different turn. Through introspection and therapy, he began to unravel the emotional legacy that fueled these patterns. His commitment to healing became a beacon of hope, illuminating a path forward for himself and future generations.

These narratives are not isolated instances but echoes of a collective human experience. The weight of history is carried in the hearts and minds of those who come after, often manifesting in subtle yet profound ways. It is a weight that can bend the branches of a family tree. Yet, it also has the potential to foster a deep sense of resilience and understanding.

As we explore these personal stories, we see that the journey within is not a solitary one. It is a shared expedition, a quest that connects us to the generations that came before and those that will follow. The legacy of trauma, while heavy, also presents an opportunity for growth and trans-formation. Through the acknowledgment and processing of this pain, healing can begin for the individual and the lineage as a whole.

Inherited family trauma is not a sentence to be served but a challenge to be met with compassion and courage. As we witness these stories, we are reminded of the strength in vulnerability and the power of confronting our inherited shadows. The journey within is a passage through time, a chance to mend the fractures of the past and forge a future where the weight of history is acknowledged, respected, and, ulti-mately, transcended.

The Quest for Identity and Belonging

In the tapestry of human experience, the threads of our ancestors' lives are interwoven with our own, often in ways we are only beginning to understand. The journey to comprehend our identity and the sense of belonging we yearn for is not merely a path we tread in isolation. It is a quest that spans generations, a search for self that reaches back into the depths of family history, where the echoes of inherited trauma reside.

The stories we carry within us are not always our own. They are endowed to us by those who came before, often passed down silently through the subtlest of behaviors, the quietest of fears, and the most unspoken of expectations. These inherited narratives shape our sense of self, our view of the world, and our place within it. They can bind us to a legacy of resilience and strength or shackle us to cycles of pain and loss that we struggle to understand, let alone break free from.

Consider Madeleine, whose grandfather survived a brutal war. He returned home a changed man, his spirit burdened with memories too painful to share. His silence was a fortress that not even his children could penetrate. Madeleine grew up in the shadow of this unspoken history, feeling the weight of an invisible inheritance. It was only when she began to explore her family's past that she realized her battles with anxiety were not solely her own but also silent whispers of her grandfather's unhealed wounds.

Then there's John, whose mother endured a tumultuous and abusive relationship. The trauma she experienced was an uninvited guest in their home, one that lingered long after the relationship ended. John learned to walk on eggshells, internalizing a sense of instability that would manifest in his relationships. It was a pattern he recognized only after embarking on a journey of self-discovery, one that led him to confront the pain his mother had inadvertently handed down to him.

These personal stories, and countless others like them, reveal the complex interplay between our quest for identity and the inherited traumas that shape our lives. They underscore the importance of understanding our family history, not to assign blame or to dwell in the past, but to gain insight into the origins of our deepest struggles. This understanding can be a powerful catalyst for healing, breaking the cycles that have held us captive, and reclaiming our life narratives.

As we delve into the layers of our family's past, we often find that our search for identity is intertwined with a need for belonging. To belong is to connect, to find our place within the continuum of our lineage, and to recognize the resilience that has carried our family through adversity. It is also to acknowledge the pain and offer compassion to those who came before us and ourselves as we grapple with the legacies we carry.

In embracing the full spectrum of our family's narrative, we can begin to forge a new sense of identity that honors our history without being confined by it. We can build a sense of belonging that is rooted not in past traumas but in the understanding and healing that the present allows. This is the essence of our quest, a deeply personal journey and inextricably linked to the generations that have paved the way for our own steps.

As we continue to navigate the intricate paths of our inner worlds, let us do so with the knowledge that our search for identity and belonging is a profound act of healing, one that has the power to transform not only our own lives but the legacy we leave for those who will follow.

Chapter Summary

- The chapter discusses the impact of inherited family trauma on individuals through personal narratives.
- Maria's story illustrates how unspoken grief from her grandfather's war experiences affected her own life.
- David's narrative shows how the chaos of his mother's abusive marriage influenced his adult relationships.
- Acknowledgment and validation of inherited trauma are presented as crucial steps toward healing.
- The chapter emphasizes the transformative power of recognizing and accepting the pain of past generations.
- Turning points and catalysts for change are highlighted as pivotal in breaking the cycle of inherited trauma.
- The weight of history and the responsibility of legacy bearers to confront and heal from past traumas are explored.
- The quest for identity and belonging is tied to understanding and healing from family history and inherited trauma.

8

PATHWAYS TO HEALING: THERAPEUTIC APPROACHES

Traditional Psychotherapy and Family Trauma

In the realm of traditional psychotherapy, the exploration and treatment of inherited family trauma necessitates a nuanced understanding of the human psyche and the intricate web of familial relationships. It is within this context that therapists often turn to time-honored approaches such as psychodynamic therapy, family systems therapy, and cognitive-behavioral therapy (CBT) to unravel the complex layers of intergenerational trauma.

Psychodynamic therapy delves into the unconscious mind, seeking to uncover the deep-seated roots of emotional suffering that may span multiple generations. It operates on the premise that the unresolved issues of our ancestors can insidiously influence our emotional landscape. Through the therapeutic alliance, individuals are encouraged to explore their family history, identifying patterns and unconscious scripts that have been passed down. This introspective journey can be both profound and challenging, as it often involves confronting painful memories and long-standing defense mechanisms.

On the other hand, family systems therapy adopts a more holistic view, considering the family as an interconnected unit where each member's behavior affects the whole. It posits that trauma is not just an individual experience but one that permeates the family system, creating ripples that can affect multiple generations. Engaging multiple family members in the therapeutic process aims to foster understanding and healing within the relational dynamics. It is through the reconfiguration of these dynamics and the establishment of healthier communication patterns that families can begin to break the cycle of trauma.

CBT, with its structured approach, offers another avenue for addressing the cognitive distortions that may arise from inherited trauma. It helps individuals recognize and challenge maladaptive thought patterns, equipping them with coping strategies and ultimately transforming their emotional responses. While CBT is often more focused on present-day symptoms and behaviors, it can still be adapted to address the historical context of these issues, providing a bridge between past traumas and current experiences.

Each of these therapeutic modalities offers unique insights and tools for healing. Yet, they share a common goal: to help individuals and families understand the origins of their pain, develop resilience, and cultivate a sense of agency over their lives. The therapeutic journey is one of reclamation as clients learn to reclaim their narratives from the shadows of the past.

As we transition from the traditional psychotherapy methods to the innovative therapies in the following section, it is essential to recognize that each approach serves as a stepping stone toward healing. The following therapies we will explore, such as Eye Movement Desensitization and Reprocessing (EMDR) and Somatic Experiencing, build upon the foundation laid by traditional methods, offering new perspectives and techniques for individuals grappling with the echoes of family trauma. While distinct in their methodologies, these modalities continue the overarching mission of traditional therapy: to facilitate a journey of healing that honors both the individual and the collective story of the family.

Innovative Therapies: EMDR, Somatic Experiencing, and More

As we delve deeper into the therapeutic approaches for inherited family trauma, it is essential to recognize the value of innovative therapies that have emerged in recent years. These modalities, while not as traditional as the psychotherapy discussed earlier, offer unique pathways to healing that may resonate with individuals for whom conventional treatments have been less effective.

Eye Movement Desensitization and Reprocessing (EMDR) is one such therapy that has garnered attention for its effectiveness in treating trauma. Developed by Francine Shapiro in the late 1980s, EMDR is predicated on the idea that the mind can heal from psychological trauma much as the body recovers from physical trauma. When a disturbing event occurs, it can get locked in the nervous system with the original pictures, sounds, thoughts, feelings, and body sensations. EMDR unlocks the nervous system and allows the mind and body to process the experience. This is particularly relevant for inherited family trauma, as it may help individuals process and integrate traumatic memories that are not directly on their own but have been passed down through generations.

EMDR involves the therapist guiding the client through a series of lateral eye movements while recalling the traumatic event, which is believed to work by mimicking the psychological state we enter during REM sleep. This state may facilitate the integration of complex memories and emotions. For those grappling with inherited family trauma, EMDR offers a way to address the complex layers of intergenerational pain without the necessity of a linear narrative, which can sometimes be elusive.

Another approach that has shown promise is somatic observing (SE), developed by Dr. Peter Levine. SE is grounded in the understanding that trauma may manifest as physical symptoms in the body. It focuses on the client's perceived body sensations (or somatic experiences) rather than solely on the cognitive or emotional aspects of trauma. By paying close attention to the body's responses, individuals learn to release and resolve the physical tension in the aftermath of traumatic events. This method can be particularly beneficial for inherited family trauma, as it addresses the often unconscious and somatically stored trauma responses that are passed down from one generation to the next.

SE therapy is a gentle and gradual process, allowing individuals to develop increased tolerance to complex bodily sensations and suppressed emotions. It is a holistic approach that not only acknowledges the psychological impact of trauma but also the bodily and instinctual dimensions of our experience. This can be a powerful method for those who carry the weight of their ancestors' traumas in their bodies, perhaps in ways they cannot fully articulate through words alone.

Beyond EMDR and SE, other innovative therapies have been developed to address trauma, such as Internal Family Systems (IFS) and Narrative Therapy. These approaches offer different lenses to view and heal from inherited family trauma, emphasizing the diversity of our inner experiences and the power of re-authoring our stories.

As we continue to explore the spectrum of therapeutic options available, it becomes clear that the journey to healing from inherited family trauma is not a one-size-fits-all endeavor. It is a deeply personal process that may require a combination of approaches, and individuals must find the path that resonates most profoundly with their unique experiences and needs. The following steps in this journey involve turning inward as we consider the role of mindfulness and meditation in fostering an environment within ourselves that is conducive to healing and growth.

The Role of Mindfulness and Meditation

In the journey toward healing inherited family trauma, we find ourselves at the crossroads of ancient wisdom and modern psychological understanding. Mindfulness and meditation, steeped in historical reverence, have emerged as powerful tools in the therapeutic landscape. Their role in addressing the wounds of the past is not merely supportive; it is transformative.

Mindfulness, the art of being fully present and engaged with the here and now without judgment, offers a profound gateway to self-awareness. For individuals grappling with the echoes of familial suffering, mindfulness provides a means to observe their internal landscape without being overwhelmed by the intensity of emotions and memories that may arise. It is a practice of cultivating a compassionate witness within oneself, a witness that acknowledges pain without becoming entangled in it.

Meditation, a companion to mindfulness, invites a deeper exploration into the self. Through various forms, from focused attention to movement-based practices, meditation allows individuals to step back from the constant chatter of the mind and the often unconscious narratives inherited from family history. In the stillness that meditation fosters, there is space for new insights to emerge—insights that can lead to the unraveling of generational patterns.

The therapeutic power of these practices lies in their ability to alter the relationship one has with one's thoughts and feelings. Research has shed light on how mindfulness and meditation can change the brain's structure and function, leading to increased emotional regulation, decreased reactivity to stress, and improved mental clarity. These neurological shifts are particularly beneficial for those whose inherited trauma has left them with a heightened stress response or a pervasive sense of anxiety.

Moreover, mindfulness and meditation do not require one to relive the traumatic events of the past, which can be retraumatizing for some. Instead, these practices encourage a gentle and gradual healing process that honors the individual's pace and capacity for growth. They empower individuals to reclaim their agency, often diminished by the weight of trauma, by offering them the skills to manage their emotional states and to make conscious choices in their thoughts and actions.

In the therapeutic setting, mindfulness and meditation can seamlessly integrate into client work. Therapists may guide individuals through mindfulness exercises during sessions, teaching them how to ground themselves in the present moment when distressing memories surface. Meditation can also be introduced as a daily practice that supports the therapeutic process by providing a consistent framework for self-reflection and emotional balance.

As we move forward in our exploration of healing modalities, it is essential to recognize the collective dimension of inherited family trauma. The following section will delve into the significance of group work and community healing, where the shared experience of trauma and recovery fosters a sense of solidarity and collective transformation. Mindfulness and meditation, while often practiced individually, can also be adapted to these communal settings, offering a shared language for understanding and healing.

Group Work and Community Healing

On the path to recovery from generational family trauma, the solitary pursuit of mindfulness and meditation can be significantly enriched by the embrace of collective experiences. Group work and community healing offer a powerful antidote to the isolation that often accompanies the deep-seated wounds of intergenerational pain. Within the safe confines of a group, individuals find solace and the shared strength to confront and reframe the narratives that have been passed down through their lineage.

The efficacy of group therapy lies in its capacity to mirror the familial and social dynamics that may have contributed to the perpetuation of trauma. Within this microcosm, individuals can explore the impact of their inherited stories, behaviors, and emotions in a space that fosters empathy and understanding. The group setting provides a platform for multiple voices, allowing participants to witness and participate in each other's healing processes, which can be profoundly validating and transformative.

One of the critical components of group work is the sense of belonging it instills. For many, realizing they are not alone in their struggles is revelatory and liberating. The shared experiences within the group can dismantle the walls of loneliness and secrecy that often surround family trauma. As members articulate their experiences and listen to others, they recognize familiar patterns and themes, which can lead to a collective sense of identity and purpose.

The role of the facilitator in this setting is to guide the process with sensitivity and expertise, ensuring that the environment remains respectful and supportive. Skilled facilitators encourage expressing emotions and exchanging perspectives while maintaining boundaries that protect the group's integrity. They help members navigate the delicate balance between personal introspection and communal interaction, fostering a space where healing can occur individually and collectively.

Community healing extends the principles of group work to a broader context, recognizing that the roots of trauma often lie in historical, cultural, or societal events. Engaging with one's community can provide a larger framework for understanding the origins of family trauma and how it has been sustained over generations. Community-based initiatives include public storytelling events, healing circles, or cultural rituals, which can validate individual experiences and promote collective catharsis.

In these communal spaces, the shared acknowledgment of past injustices and the commitment to breaking cycles of pain can be a potent force for change. Here, individuals can find a sense of agency, learning to advocate for their own healing and the transformation of the community as a whole. The collective endeavor to heal can lead to new traditions and practices that honor the past while actively shaping a more conscious and compassionate future.

As we delve deeper into the therapeutic approaches to inherited family trauma, it becomes clear that the integration of group work and community healing is not just beneficial but essential. The collective journey mirrors our own experiences and offers a window into the shared human condition, reminding us that our stories are interconnected and that our healing, too, is a shared responsibility.

Integrating New Narratives

In the journey toward healing from inherited family trauma, we have explored the power of collective experiences through group work and the solidarity found within community healing. As we transition from the shared to the personal, we delve into individual narratives and the profound impact of integrating new, empowering stories into one's life.

The human psyche is akin to a tapestry woven with the threads of our experiences, beliefs, and the stories we tell ourselves about who we are and where we come from. For those carrying the weight of inherited trauma, the narrative often includes themes of pain, loss, and a sense of certainty that the past seals one's fate. However, integrating new narratives offers hope, illuminating the path to rewriting one's story with autonomy and resilience.

The therapeutic approach to integrating new narratives begins with acknowledging the existing story. It requires a compassionate and empathetic exploration of the trauma narrative passed down through generations. This understanding is not to dwell on the suffering but to recognize its influence on the individual's life script. By bringing these stories into the light, we can see them not as unchangeable truths but as narratives that have been shaped by many hands and can be reshaped by the one holding the pen now.

The next step is the deliberate and often challenging work of crafting a new narrative. This is not about denying or erasing the past but expanding the story to include the strength, survival, and lessons learned from ancestors' experiences. It is about recognizing that while the trauma is a part of history, it does not have to dictate the future. Individuals are encouraged to identify and amplify their values, aspirations, and dreams, weaving these into the fabric of their new narrative.

Therapists may use various techniques to facilitate this process, such as narrative therapy, which involves re-authoring one's story, or cognitive-behavioral approaches that help to reframe and challenge unhelpful beliefs. Creative expression also serves as a powerful tool, allowing for the externalization of the trauma narrative and the active construction of a new one through art, writing, or drama.

As individuals begin to integrate these new narratives, they often experience a shift in their identity. They start to see themselves not as victims of their family's past but as active agents in their own lives. This redefined self-concept opens up possibilities for healing within themselves, their relationships, and the broader family system. The new narrative becomes a legacy of its own, one that can be passed down to future generations, marked not by the scars of trauma but by the resilience and conscious creation of a hopeful future.

Integrating new narratives is a profound act of reclamation and transformation. It is a testament to the human capacity for change and the power of stories to shape our reality. As we continue to explore the pathways to healing, we recognize that each individual's journey is unique. Yet, there is a universal thread that connects us all—the enduring ability to rewrite our stories and, in doing so, to reclaim our lives.

Chapter Summary

- Traditional psychotherapy approaches like psychodynamic therapy, family systems therapy, and CBT are used to address inherited family trauma.
- Psychodynamic therapy explores the unconscious mind to uncover emotional suffering that may span generations.
- Family systems therapy views the family as an interconnected unit and addresses trauma as a shared experience within this system.
- CBT focuses on present-day symptoms and behaviors, helping individuals recognize and challenge maladaptive thought patterns.
- Innovative therapies like EMDR and Somatic Experiencing offer new techniques for dealing with intergenerational trauma.

- EMDR facilitates the processing of traumatic memories through eye movements, while SE focuses on resolving physical tension related to trauma.
- Mindfulness and meditation are transformative practices that help individuals manage their emotional states and foster self-awareness.
- Group work and community healing provide a collective space for individuals to share their experiences and find solidarity in their journey toward healing.

9

THE RIPPLE EFFECT: RELATIONSHIPS AND SOCIETY

Interpersonal Relationships and Trauma Patterns

Within relationships, the threads of inherited family trauma are often woven so subtly into the fabric of our interactions that they can go unnoticed, yet their influence is profound. These inherited patterns of behavior and emotional responses passed down from one generation to the next can shape the dynamics of our closest relationships in complex and far-reaching ways.

The concept of inherited family trauma suggests that the unresolved traumas of our ancestors do not simply vanish with time. Instead, they linger, silently scripting the emotional landscapes of those who follow. This can manifest in a myriad of ways within interpersonal relationships. For instance, a parent who experienced abandonment as a child may, despite their best intentions, struggle with attachment issues, inadvertently creating a sense of insecurity in their children. Similarly, a partner who has inherited a legacy of mistrust may find it challenging to cultivate a healthy, trusting relationship with their spouse.

These patterns are not merely psychological but can be deeply embedded in the nonverbal cues and emotional responses integral to human connection. The way one might flinch at a raised voice or the difficulty another might have in expressing affection can be echoes of past traumas that were never fully processed or understood by the individuals who first experienced them. It is through these unspoken languages that the legacy of trauma is often most powerfully transmitted.

The impact of such inherited trauma on relationships can be profound. It can lead to cycles of dysfunction, where individuals unwittingly recreate the emotional environments that were modeled to them in childhood. This can result in a cascade of relational challenges, including communication breakdowns, emotional volatility, and a pervasive sense of disconnection. Even more insidiously, these patterns can become normalized within families, creating a blueprint for relationships that is difficult to recognize as harmful because it is so familiar.

However, it is essential to approach this subject not with resignation but with a sense of empowered awareness. Recognizing these patterns is the first step in breaking the cycle. It allows individuals to understand that their struggles within relationships may not be solely of their own making but rather part of a larger historical context. This understanding can foster empathy for oneself and family members grappling with the legacy of past traumas.

By bringing these patterns into the light, individuals and families can begin the work of healing. This often involves developing a new emotional vocabulary that includes the language of validation, understanding, and resilience. It may also require the support of therapeutic interventions that specifically address the complexities of inherited trauma, helping individuals to disentangle their emotional responses from those of their ancestors.

As we delve deeper into the understanding of how inherited family trauma shapes our relationships, we pave the way for more conscious and intentional interactions. This journey of awareness and healing is about looking back and moving forward with a new sense of clarity and purpose. It is about rewriting the emotional scripts handed down to us and choosing to foster relationships rooted in health, understanding, and compassion.

In this pursuit of transformation, the role of community cannot be understated. It is within the collective embrace of a trauma-informed society that individuals find the strength and support to heal not only themselves but also the relational fabric that binds us all. As we transition to exploring the concept of trauma-informed communities, we carry with us the understanding that healing inherited family trauma is not a solitary endeavor but a communal one, where the collective wisdom and compassion of the community play an integral role in facilitating individual and familial healing.

Trauma-Informed Communities

When discussing human relationships and societal structures, the silent threads of inherited family trauma weave through generations, often unnoticed yet profoundly influential. As we delve into the concept of trauma-informed communities, we recognize that these are not merely clusters of individuals but ecosystems of interconnected lives, where the health and resilience of one part invariably affect the whole.

A trauma-informed community acknowledges the pervasive impact of trauma and understands potential paths for recovery. It recognizes the signs and symptoms of trauma in individuals, families, and groups. It integrates this knowledge into its practices and policies. In doing so, it actively seeks to resist re-traumatization and to foster a supportive environment where healing can occur.

The foundation of such a community lies in empathy and education. Empathy, the ability to understand and share the feelings of another, is the cornerstone of a trauma-informed approach. It requires us to look beyond individuals' immediate behaviors and circumstances and consider the complex interplay of historical, emotional, and psychological factors that contribute to their current state.

Education, on the other hand, equips community members with the knowledge to recognize the signs of inherited trauma. It enables them to respond appropriately, whether it be through providing support, advocating for resources, or simply offering a listening ear. Education also serves to destigmatize the experiences of those affected by trauma, fostering a culture of openness and acceptance.

In practice, a trauma-informed community operates on several principles. Safety is paramount—both physical and emotional. People need to feel secure before they can begin to address the wounds of the past. Trustworthiness is also crucial, as it lays the groundwork for meaningful connections and the belief that change is possible.

Collaboration and mutuality are the lifeblood of a trauma-informed community. Healing from trauma is rarely a solitary journey; it thrives on the mutual support and shared experiences of others. Empowerment, voice, and choice are also essential, as they restore a sense of control and agency to those who may feel dispossessed by their inherited burdens.

In such communities, service providers and community leaders are not to act as distant authorities but as healing facilitators. They empower individuals and families, helping them navigate the complexities of their experiences and find their own paths to wellness. This approach requires a shift from asking "What's wrong with you?" to "What happened to you?"—a subtle yet profound change in perspective that honors the individual's story and strength.

Moreover, trauma-informed communities are proactive in their approach to intergenerational healing. They invest in programs and initiatives that address the root causes of trauma, such as poverty, discrimination, and violence. They also strive to create opportunities for positive experiences and relationships that can counterbalance the effects of past traumas.

The ripple effect of such an approach is far-reaching. When a community becomes trauma-informed, it not only aids in the healing of those directly affected by inherited family trauma but also contributes to the overall well-being of all its members. It becomes a place where cycles of pain are interrupted and replaced with cycles of growth and resilience.

As we look towards the horizon of a more compassionate and understanding society, we see the emergence of trauma-informed communities as beacons of hope. They stand as a testament to our collective ability to confront the shadows of the past and to lay the groundwork for a future where the legacy of trauma is acknowledged, addressed, and transformed into a source of collective strength.

Education and Awareness: Breaking the Stigma

Inherited family trauma is not merely a personal struggle; it casts a long shadow across generations, influencing relationships and the very fabric of society. Yet, despite its pervasive nature, there remains a profound stigma attached to the acknowledgment and discussion of such trauma. This stigma acts as a barrier, preventing individuals from seeking the support they need and society from offering the understanding necessary for healing.

Breaking this stigma requires a multifaceted approach, with education and awareness at its core. It is essential to foster a culture where the complexities of inherited trauma are recognized and addressed with compassion rather than judgment. This begins with transforming our educational systems to include comprehensive mental health education that encompasses the nuances of inherited trauma.

By integrating this topic into school curriculums, we can equip the next generation with a better understanding of the psychological and emotional legacies that can be passed down through families. This education should not only focus on the symptoms and mechanisms of inherited trauma but also emphasize resilience, coping strategies, and the importance of seeking help. Such an approach can empower young people to break cycles of trauma, fostering healthier relationships and communities.

Moreover, awareness campaigns play a pivotal role in changing public perception. These campaigns should aim to normalize conversations about mental health and inherited trauma, highlighting personal stories and scientific research. By bringing these narratives into the public domain, we can challenge misconceptions and create a more empathetic society that encourages healing and support.

Healthcare professionals also have a significant role in breaking the stigma. Training for doctors, therapists, and social workers should include modules on the identification and treatment of inherited trauma. A well-informed healthcare provider can offer appropriate support and validate a patient's experiences, which is a crucial step in destigmatizing the issue.

In addition to formal education and professional training, the media has a powerful influence on public opinion. Responsible reporting and storytelling can contribute to a more informed and sensitive portrayal of inherited trauma. Media professionals should be encouraged to engage with experts and those affected by inherited trauma to ensure that their stories are told with accuracy and dignity.

Breaking the stigma surrounding inherited family trauma is not an overnight task. It requires a concerted effort from educators, healthcare providers, policymakers, the media, and society. By fostering an environment of openness and education, we can create a supportive space for individuals to share their experiences without fear of judgment. In doing so, we pave the way for healing within families and within the broader societal tapestry woven from the threads of our collective experiences.

Policy and Advocacy: Social Change

In the quest to understand inherited family trauma, we have journeyed through the corridors of personal experience and societal perception. We've explored the profound impact that unaddressed trauma can have on individuals and the relationships they nurture. As we turn our attention to the broader societal implications, it becomes clear that the path to healing is not just a private endeavor but a collective one, requiring policy and advocacy to forge social change.

The acknowledgment of inherited family trauma as a significant factor in the well-being of individuals and communities has been slow to permeate the halls of legislation and public policy. Yet, the need for such recognition is critical. Through the lens of policy, society can shift from a reactive stance to a proactive one, implementing strategies that address the symptoms of trauma, its root causes, and intergenerational transmission.

Advocacy plays a pivotal role in this transformation. Advocates for mental health and trauma-informed care are the voices that can articulate the silent struggles of countless individuals, bringing their stories to the forefront of public consciousness. They serve as the bridge between personal narratives and policy-making, translating the complex language of trauma into actionable items that can be enshrined in law and practice.

One of the most significant steps in policy and advocacy is the integration of trauma-informed approaches into all sectors of society. This means training educators, healthcare providers, law enforcement, and social services personnel to recognize the signs of inherited trauma and to respond with empathy and effective interventions. It requires a shift in perspective from punitive measures to supportive ones, recognizing that behaviors often stem from cycles of trauma.

Moreover, policy initiatives must provide accessible and affordable mental health resources to all population segments. This includes funding for research into the effects of inherited trauma and the development of targeted therapies to halt the cycle. It also involves creating community-based programs that offer support and education to families dealing with the repercussions of past traumas.

In advocating for these changes, it is essential to engage with those who have lived experiences of inherited trauma. Their insights are invaluable in shaping well-informed but also compassionate and effective policies. Policies that genuinely resonate with the needs of those they are meant to serve can be crafted by involving survivors in the conversation.

Furthermore, policy and advocacy must also address the broader societal conditions that perpetuate trauma. This includes tackling systemic issues such as poverty, discrimination, and violence, which can all contribute to the cycle of trauma within families. By creating a more equitable and just society, we reduce the stressors that exacerbate inherited trauma and create an environment where healing can flourish.

The journey toward social change is undoubtedly complex, but it is also filled with hope. Each policy enacted, each advocate who raises their voice, and each professionally trained in trauma-informed care contributes to a society that not only recognizes the deep-seated impact of inherited family trauma but also commits to healing it. Through these collective efforts, we can envision a future where the ripple effect of trauma is met with a tide of support, understanding, and transformation —a legacy of healing that benefits not just individuals and families but society as a whole.

Creating a Legacy of Healing

In the wake of understanding how policy and advocacy can be leveraged to address the widespread impact of inherited family trauma, we find ourselves at a crossroads of personal responsibility and collective healing. The journey from recognizing the existence of such trauma to actively engaging in the creation of a legacy of healing is both intimate and communal. The path demands courage, compassion, and a deep commitment to transformation.

Creating a legacy of healing begins within the intricate web of our relationships. It is in the day-to-day interactions with family, friends, and partners that the patterns of inherited trauma often reveal themselves. These patterns, woven into the fabric of our interactions, can either perpetuate pain cycles or become the threads from which we weave a tapestry of recovery.

To embark on this transformative journey, we must cultivate a profound self-awareness. This involves a willingness to delve into past narratives, hold them up to the light of our consciousness, and discern the threads of trauma that may be influencing our present behaviors and choices. It is not an easy task; it requires vulnerability and a willingness to confront uncomfortable truths. Yet, through this process, we can begin to untangle the knots of our inherited stories and reclaim the agency to write new chapters.

As we engage in this personal work, we must also focus on the societal structures that hold these traumas in place. Healing is not solely an individual endeavor but inextricably linked to the collective. The environments in which we live, work, and play all contribute to either the perpetuation or the healing of inherited trauma. By advocating for compassionate and trauma-informed practices within our communities and institutions, we can create spaces that acknowledge the pain of the past and foster resilience and healing.

Moreover, the act of healing is not a solitary one. It thrives in the presence of empathetic witnesses who can hold space for our stories without judgment. This means building connections rooted in mutual respect, active listening, and emotional support in relationships. Through these relationships, we can find the strength to confront our inherited traumas and the support to navigate the complex journey of healing.

As we forge these bonds, we must also be mindful of the legacy we wish to leave for future generations. The choices we make, how we heal, and the relationships we nurture all have the potential to either reinforce the cycle of trauma or break it. By consciously choosing to heal, we are transforming our lives and shaping the inheritance we pass on to our children and their children after them.

In creating a legacy of healing, we are tasked with envisioning a future where the scars of the past no longer dictate the possibilities of the present. It is a future where each individual has the opportunity to thrive, unburdened by the weight of unspoken histories. It is a future built on the foundation of healed relationships and a society that values the wholeness of every person.

The work of healing inherited family trauma is both a personal journey and a societal imperative. It is a process that unfolds over time, with each step forward contributing to a more significant movement towards wholeness. As we engage in this work, we are reclaiming our own lives and contributing to creating a more compassionate and resilient world. It is a profound responsibility and a profound gift—a legacy of healing that can ripple through generations, transforming pain into purpose and despair into hope.

Chapter Summary

- Inherited family trauma can subtly influence interpersonal relationships, affecting behavior and emotional responses across generations.
- Trauma patterns can manifest in nonverbal cues and emotional reactions, often transmitted through unspoken languages within families.
- These inherited patterns can lead to dysfunctional relationship cycles, normalizing harmful behaviors due to familiarity.
- Recognizing inherited trauma patterns is crucial for breaking the cycle, fostering empathy, and beginning the healing process.
- Healing involves developing new emotional vocabularies and may require therapeutic interventions to address the complexities of inherited trauma.
- Trauma-informed communities acknowledge the impact of trauma and integrate this understanding into their practices and policies, fostering a supportive environment for healing.
- Education and awareness campaigns are crucial to breaking the stigma around inherited family trauma, normalizing discussions, and promoting understanding.
- Policy and advocacy are essential for societal change, requiring the integration of trauma-informed approaches across sectors and addressing systemic issues that perpetuate trauma.

10

THE NEXT GENERATION: PARENTING WITH AWARENESS

Conscious Parenting: Breaking the Cycle

In the journey of parenting, the concept of consciousness extends far beyond a child's immediate physical and emotional needs. It delves into the profound responsibility of nurturing a future adult who is not only resilient but also psychologically sound. This task becomes particularly challenging when parents themselves are the bearers of inherited family trauma. The shadows of the past, often silent and unseen, can stretch out their fingers to touch the lives of the next generation in subtle and profound ways.

Breaking the cycle of inherited family trauma is akin to tending a garden that has been neglected; it requires patience, understanding, and a willingness to delve into the soil of one's own experiences. Conscious parenting is being present with one's children, but it is also about being present with oneself. It is about recognizing the patterns handed down, perhaps through generations, and deliberately choosing not to pass them on.

To embark on this journey, parents must first acknowledge the existence of these patterns. It is not uncommon for individuals to carry the emotional baggage of their ancestors without realizing it. These can manifest as fears, anxieties, and reactions that seem disproportionate to the events that trigger them. By identifying these echoes from the past, parents can begin to understand how their behavior might be influenced by unresolved trauma.

Once acknowledged, the process of healing can begin. This is not a journey that one can undertake alone; it often requires the support of professionals who can guide and facilitate the healing process. Therapy, support groups, and other resources can provide the tools necessary to unpack the weight of the past. As parents work through their traumas, they become more capable of providing their children with a stable and nurturing environment.

But conscious parenting is not just about healing old wounds; it's also about fostering an environment where new, healthy patterns can emerge. This involves creating a space where children feel safe to express their emotions and where those emotions are met with empathy and understanding. It is about setting firm yet flexible boundaries, providing structure without stifling the child's individuality.

In this nurturing space, children learn to recognize and articulate their feelings. They are allowed to develop emotional intelligence, which is the ability to be aware of, control, and express their emotions and handle interpersonal relationships judiciously and empathetically. This skill is invaluable, laying the foundation for a lifetime of healthy relationships and emotional well-being.

Conscious parenting also requires a commitment to self-reflection. Parents must be willing to look at their responses and consider how their histories might influence them. It is a practice of asking oneself, "Is my reaction to my child's behavior about what they are doing now, or is it a response to something that happened in my past?" By staying mindful of these distinctions, parents can respond to their children in ways that are appropriate to the present moment rather than being colored by the past.

In breaking the cycle of inherited family trauma, parents give their children a precious gift: the chance to live a life that is not predetermined by the pains of previous generations. The path requires courage and commitment, but the rewards are immeasurable. Not only does it free the child to forge their path, but it also allows the parent to heal and grow in ways they may never have thought possible.

As we move forward, it is essential to consider how the principles of conscious parenting can be applied to foster attachment and emotional intelligence. These are the cornerstones upon which children can build a life that is not only free from the burdens of the past but also rich in emotional depth and understanding.

Attachment and Emotional Intelligence

During the delicate process of raising children, the silent echoes of the past often reverberate through the generations, manifesting as inherited family trauma. The imprints of these ancestral echoes can shape the emotional landscape of the next generation, often without conscious awareness. As we navigate the delicate terrain of raising children, we must foster secure attachments and cultivate emotional intelligence, both of which serve as bulwarks against the perpetuation of familial wounds.

Attachment, the deep and enduring emotional bond that connects one person to another across time and space, is the cornerstone of a child's early development. Through this primal connection, a child learns to perceive the world as either a safe haven or a landscape fraught with unpredictability. Parents attuned to their children's needs, who respond with warmth and consistency, lay the groundwork for secure attachment. This secure base is not merely a sanctuary of comfort but also a launching pad from which children can explore their environment with confidence and curiosity.

However, for parents who have themselves been the bearers of inherited trauma, the capacity to provide this secure base can be compromised. Their attachment histories, possibly marred by the shadows of unresolved pain, can inadvertently color their attachment styles to their children. It is here that the cycle of trauma finds its potential perpetuation. Yet, it is also here that the cycle can be interrupted.

Emotional intelligence, the ability to understand and manage one's emotions, as well as to empathize with the emotions of others, is a beacon that guides this interruption. Parents who consciously work on developing their emotional intelligence are better equipped to recognize and regulate their emotional responses. They can discern the subtle difference between reacting from a place of historical hurt and responding from a place of present-moment awareness.

By cultivating emotional intelligence, parents can model for their children how to navigate the complex tapestry of human emotions. Children, in turn, learn to articulate their feelings, understand the emotional cues of others, and develop empathy. This emotional literacy becomes the language through which they can communicate their inner worlds, build meaningful relationships, and engage with life's challenges with resilience.

Moreover, emotional intelligence allows parents to hold space for their children's emotions without being overwhelmed by their own. It enables them to approach their children's distress with compassion rather than anxiety, curiosity, and control. In doing so, they offer their children a relationship where emotions are not feared but are understood as signals, as messengers of needs and desires.

As we embark on parenting with awareness, we are not merely raising children but nurturing the seeds of emotional health that will flourish for generations to come. We are rewriting the narrative of our lineage, transforming inherited trauma into inherited wisdom. In this transformation lies the hope for our children to live lives unencumbered by the weight of the past, empowered to craft their own stories with intention and grace.

Teaching Resilience and Coping Skills

On the gentle path of raising children, the awareness of inherited family trauma serves as a compass, guiding us toward nurturing environments that foster resilience and equip our children with practical coping skills. As we delve into the heart of this nurturing, it is essential to understand that the ability to bounce back from adversity is not an innate trait but a skill that can be cultivated and strengthened over time.

Resilience is often misconstrued as a stoic endurance of hardship. Still, in its essence, it is the graceful dance of adapting to change, recovering from setbacks, and learning from each experience. It is about developing a core of inner strength that can be drawn upon in times of need. To instill this quality in the next generation, we must first embody it ourselves, for children are astute observers, learning more from what they witness than what they are told.

One of the most profound ways to teach resilience is through modeling. When parents face their challenges with hope and a problem-solving mindset, they provide a live blueprint for their children to emulate. It is not the absence of struggle that is most instructive but how we navigate it. By sharing our thought processes, embracing our emotions, and demonstrating perseverance, we communicate to our children that difficulties are a part of life and that they possess the capacity to overcome them.

Coping skills are the tools and strategies that individuals use to manage stress and emotional upheaval. These skills are as varied as the individuals who employ them. Yet, certain practices have been universally shown to be effective. Mindfulness, for instance, is a practice that roots us in the present moment and allows us to observe our thoughts and feelings without judgment. By teaching our children mindfulness, we give them the gift of self-awareness, which is the first step in emotional regulation.

Another vital coping skill is emotional expression. Encouraging children to articulate their feelings through conversation, art, or play helps them process their emotions. It reduces the likelihood of these feelings manifesting in harmful ways. Parents need to create a safe space where emotions are not only allowed but welcomed. This openness paves the way for children to seek support and guidance when struggling rather than bottling up their feelings.

Problem-solving is a skill that empowers children to take active steps in confronting their challenges. Children learn that they have agency in their lives by breaking down problems into manageable pieces, considering various solutions, and evaluating outcomes. Parents can foster this skill by involving their children in discussions about family challenges, allowing them to offer input and, when appropriate, letting them experience the natural consequences of their choices.

In addition to these practices, it is crucial to recognize the role of social support in building resilience. Relationships with family, friends, and community members provide a network of care that can buffer against the effects of stress and trauma. Teaching children to cultivate and maintain these relationships ensures they can access diverse perspectives and resources when facing challenges.

As we journey forward, it is with the understanding that resilience and coping skills are not static qualities but dynamic processes that evolve with experience. Our role as parents is not to shield our children from every hardship but to prepare them to meet life's complexities with courage, adaptability, and an open heart. In doing so, we help to break the cycle of inherited family trauma, paving the way for a future where each generation is stronger and more emotionally intelligent than the last.

The Role of Education and Support

As we navigate the complex landscape of parenting in the shadow of inherited family trauma, it becomes increasingly clear that education and support play pivotal roles in shaping the future of the next generation. The task at hand is not only to break the cycle of trauma but to nurture an environment where children can thrive, unencumbered by the burdens of the past.

To this end, parents need to seek out and engage with educational resources that provide insight into the nature of inherited trauma. Knowledge is a powerful tool in this journey. Understanding how trauma can be transmitted across generations enables parents to identify patterns that may be present in their family history. This awareness is the first step toward change.

However, education extends beyond the theoretical understanding of trauma. It involves learning practical strategies for creating a stable and nurturing home environment. Parenting programs and workshops can offer valuable guidance on fostering secure attachment, emotional intelligence, and open communication. These skills empower parents to become the architects of a new family legacy that champions emotional health and resilience.

Support systems are equally crucial. The journey of healing and transformation can be arduous and lonely without a network of understanding individuals who can offer empathy, encouragement, and advice. Support groups, whether in-person or online, provide a communal space for parents to share experiences, challenges, and triumphs. Within these groups, parents often find solace in the shared understanding that they are not alone in their struggles.

Moreover, professional support from therapists or counselors trained in dealing with family trauma can be instrumental. These professionals can guide parents through the process of unpacking their trauma, learning how to manage its impact, and developing strategies to prevent its transmission to their children. They can also assist in addressing any signs of trauma that may already be manifesting in children, providing early intervention that can alter the course of a child's life.

It is essential to recognize that education and support are not static resources but dynamic processes that evolve as a family grows and changes. As children develop, new challenges and questions arise, necessitating a continuous commitment to learning and seeking support. This ongoing engagement is a testament to the resilience of the human spirit and its capacity for growth and transformation.

In the context of inherited family trauma, the role of education and support is not merely to inform or to console—it is to empower. It is to equip parents with the tools they need to rewrite the narratives of their lives and, in doing so, to lay the groundwork for their children to build their own stories, free from the echoes of trauma. This empowerment is the foundation upon which hope and positive futures are built, ensuring that the legacy passed down to the next generation is one of strength, understanding, and boundless potential.

Fostering Hope and Positive Futures

In the delicate dance of parenting, the awareness of inherited family trauma is akin to a subtle undercurrent that can guide the steps of those involved. It is a silent narrative that, if left unaddressed, can repeat its patterns through generations. However, when parents approach their role with a conscious understanding of this phenomenon, they can change the rhythm and foster hope and positive futures for their children.

The task is not to eradicate the past—our histories are indelible parts of us—but to cultivate an environment where the past does not dictate the future. It is about nurturing resilience and equipping the next generation with the tools to survive and thrive despite the shadows that may loom from familial experiences.

To achieve this, parents can adopt a proactive stance that emphasizes the strengths and potential of their children. This involves recognizing each child as an individual separate from the family's traumatic narrative. It is about celebrating their unique qualities and encouraging their personal growth and development, free from the constraints of inherited burdens.

Creating open lines of communication is paramount. Children should feel safe to express their emotions, fears, and dreams. By fostering a household where dialogue about feelings and experiences is normalized, parents can help their children develop emotional intelligence and resilience. This practice also serves as a preventive measure, ensuring that children do not internalize stress or trauma as their predecessors might have.

Moreover, instilling a sense of hope and optimism in children is essential. This can be achieved through positive reinforcement, highlighting their achievements, and supporting their ambitions. It is also important to model coping strategies emphasizing adaptability and problem-solving, showing children that challenges can be met with creativity and determination.

In addition, parents can encourage their children to engage with the world around them, fostering connections with peers, mentors, and communities. These relationships can provide support systems outside of the family unit, offering diverse perspectives and experiences that can enrich a child's worldview and sense of belonging.

Lastly, parents need to engage in self-care and personal development. By addressing their traumas and emotional needs, parents can break the transmission cycle and present a healthier model of coping and living for their children to emulate. This self-work is not a selfish act but a profound investment in the well-being of future generations.

In conclusion, parenting with awareness of inherited family trauma is a journey that requires intention, compassion, and a forward-looking perspective. It is about creating a legacy not of repeated patterns but of conscious growth and healing. By fostering hope and optimistic futures, parents can empower their children to write stories that honor the past but are not bound by it.

Chapter Summary

- Conscious parenting involves nurturing a psychologically sound future adult and breaking the cycle of inherited family trauma.
- Parents must acknowledge and understand their inherited patterns to prevent passing them on to their children.
- Healing from inherited trauma often requires professional support, such as therapy, to provide a stable environment for children.
- Conscious parenting includes creating a safe space for emotional expression and fostering emotional intelligence in children.

- Parents need to practice self-reflection to ensure their reactions to their children are present-focused and not influenced by past trauma.
- Secure attachment and emotional intelligence are crucial to preventing the perpetuation of familial wounds and fostering resilience.
- Education and support systems, including parenting programs and professional counseling, are crucial for parents dealing with inherited trauma.
- Fostering hope and positive futures involves recognizing each child's individuality, open communication, and parents' self-care and personal development.

EMBRACING OUR COLLECTIVE JOURNEY

Reflecting on Our Shared Humanity

As we draw near the close of this exploration into the depths of inherited family trauma, it is essential to pause and consider the profound interconnectedness that binds us all. The tapestry of our lives is woven with threads of experiences passed down through generations, each strand colored with the hues of joy, pain, resilience, and hope. Recognizing our shared humanity, we find the strength to confront the shadows of our collective past and the courage to illuminate the path forward.

Inherited trauma is not a solitary journey. It is a shared narrative that crosses the boundaries of time, culture, and geography. The silent echo of our ancestors' struggles resonates within us, shaping our beliefs, behaviors, and the essence of our being. Yet, within this echo lies a universal truth: we are more alike than different. Our capacity to feel pain and heal is a testament to the indomitable spirit that resides within us.

As we reflect on the stories that have been shared, the insights gleaned, and the wisdom imparted, we understand that acknowledging our vulnerabilities is not a sign of weakness but a courageous act of authenticity. Through this vulnerability, we invite connection, understanding, and healing. By recognizing the fragments of ourselves in the experiences of others, we begin to dismantle the barriers that have kept us isolated in our suffering.

The journey of healing inherited family trauma is not one that we undertake alone. It is a collective endeavor that requires us to extend our hands in solidarity, to offer our shoulders for others to lean on, and to open our hearts to the stories that have shaped us. It is a process that demands empathy, not just for others but for ourselves, for it is in the gentle embrace of self-compassion that we find the space to grow, change, and break the cycles that have held us captive.

In embracing our shared humanity, we recognize that the path to healing is not linear. It is a mosaic of experiences, a constellation of moments with the potential for growth and transformation. We learn to celebrate the small victories, cherish the incremental steps toward wholeness, and honor the resilience that has carried us through the darkest times.

As we stand at the precipice of new beginnings, let us carry with us the knowledge that our stories do not end with us. They ripple outwards, touching the lives of those yet to come. It is our responsibility, our privilege, to pave the way for a future where the chains of inherited trauma are broken and where the next generation can flourish unencumbered by the weight of the past.

In the stillness of introspection, let us hold space for the healing yet to unfold, the stories yet to be told, and the collective journey that we continue to navigate. Together, with compassion as our compass and empathy as our guide, we step into a world where our shared humanity is the beacon that lights the way to a brighter, more connected future.

The Power of Compassion and Empathy

As we conclude our exploration of inherited family trauma, we come to recognize a profound truth: the healing journey is not one we walk alone. It is a path paved with the collective efforts of every individual who dares to confront the echoes of the past. In this recognition, we find the power of compassion and empathy to be therapeutic tools and vital human connections that bind us in our quest for understanding and peace.

Compassion, in its purest form, is an emotional response that arises from witnessing another's suffering, coupled with a genuine desire to alleviate it. When we apply compassion to inherited family trauma, we extend our hearts to those who came before us and ourselves and our descendants. It is an acknowledgment that the wounds we carry are not singular in their existence; they are shared across generations, and thus, our compassion must be expansive and inclusive.

Empathy, the ability to understand and share the feelings of another, is the bridge that connects our own experiences with those of our ancestors. Empathy allows us to feel the weight of their stories and acknowledge the burden of their unhealed traumas without judgment or reservation. Through this empathetic connection, we begin to unravel the complex tapestry of our family's emotional legacy.

The power of these twin forces—compassion and empathy—lies in their ability to transform our perspective. They encourage us to look beyond the surface of our inherited narratives to see the vulnerabilities and strengths passed down through time. They ask us to consider the resilience of the human spirit and the capacity for renewal that resides within each of us.

In embracing compassion and empathy, we also embrace a form of radical acceptance. This acceptance does not mean condoning the painful events of the past or the behaviors that arose from them. Instead, it is an acknowledgment of their reality, an understanding that to move forward, we must first accept where we are and where we have come from. It is a gentle but firm assertion that we are not defined by our trauma but by how we respond to it.

As we cultivate these qualities within ourselves, we also foster a more compassionate and empathetic society. We become advocates for healing within the confines of our own families and within the broader human family. We recognize that the threads of trauma are interwoven in the fabric of our collective history and that by pulling on one, we have the chance to unravel them all.

In this space of shared vulnerability and mutual support, we find the courage to confront the shadows of the past. We learn to hold space for each other's stories, to listen deeply, and to respond with kindness. Here, in the heart of compassion and empathy, we discover the potential for profound transformation—not as isolated individuals but as a united community bound by the common threads of our human experience.

As we stand on the threshold of this understanding, we prepare to step into the wisdom of healing, carrying with us the lessons of compassion and empathy as guiding lights on our collective journey.

The Wisdom of Healing

As we approach the end of our exploration into the depths of inherited family trauma, we arrive at a place of profound understanding—a place where the wisdom of healing begins to illuminate our path. This wisdom, often hard-earned through the trials of personal experience and collective suffering, offers a beacon of hope that guides us toward a future less burdened by the echoes of our ancestors' pain.

The journey of healing is not a solitary one. It is a tapestry woven from the threads of our shared humanity, colored by the diverse experiences we bring to the loom. In recognizing the interconnectedness of our stories, we find strength. It is a strength that comes not from isolation but from the collective courage to face the shadows of our familial pasts and the determination to transform them into the light for future generations.

Healing inherited family trauma requires us to delve into the innermost chambers of our hearts to confront the fears and vulnerabilities that reside there. It is a process that demands honesty, not just with ourselves but also our lineage. As we embark on this introspective journey, we learn that the wisdom of healing is not about erasing the past but about understanding its influence on our present and reshaping its impact on our future.

This wisdom teaches us that healing is an act of reclamation. It is about reclaiming our narratives, our identities, and our rightful place within the continuum of our family's history. It is about acknowledging the suffering that has been endured while also recognizing the resilience that has allowed us to survive and, indeed, to thrive. Through this reclamation, we begin to dissolve the barriers that trauma has erected between us and our potential for growth and fulfillment.

The wisdom of healing also brings with it the recognition that we are not just the sum of our inherited pain. We also carry our ancestors' dreams, hopes, and unfulfilled aspirations. In healing, we honor their legacy not by perpetuating their traumas but by nurturing the seeds of possibility they planted, often unconsciously, within us. We become the custodians of a new legacy—one defined by healing, empowerment, and the promise of a future unshackled from the chains of the past.

As we embrace this wisdom, we find that the healing process is not linear. It ebbs and flows like the tides, with moments of profound insight and periods of quiet reflection. Each step forward is an act of bravery, a testament to the human spirit's capacity for renewal and transformation. And with each step, we weave a new pattern into the fabric of our lives, one that honors the complexity of our heritage while forging a path toward a more conscious and compassionate existence.

In this space of healing, we are not alone. We stand shoulder to shoulder with those who have walked this path before us and those who will follow in our footsteps. Together, we are part of a collective journey that transcends time and space, uniting us in a shared quest for understanding, peace, and a world where the wisdom of healing is not just an aspiration but a reality for all.

The Horizon of Possibility

As we stand on the precipice of understanding, gazing into the vast expanse of what could be, we must recognize the power of possibility that lies before us. The journey of grappling with inherited family trauma is not a path walked in isolation. It is a collective expedition that we navigate together as a society enriched by diverse experiences and united by a common desire for healing and growth.

The horizon of possibility stretches out, inviting us to envision a future where the chains of intergenerational pain are acknowledged and actively dismantled. It is a future where the narratives of our ancestors become lessons of resilience rather than scripts for suffering. In this envisioned world, the wisdom gleaned from our forebears' trials is transformed into a roadmap for emotional liberation and well-being.

Imagine a society that embraces the complexity of its history, where the stories of our lineage are not sources of shame but wellsprings of strength. In this society, children are born into environments conscious of the past but not confined by it. Parents and guardians are equipped with the tools to not only heal their wounds but also to prevent the transmission of trauma to the next generation.

The science of epigenetics has shown us that our genes are not our destiny. They are dynamic and responsive to the environments we create and the experiences we undergo. This knowledge empowers us to be architects of our genetic expression and to choose paths of healing that can reverberate through our DNA and echo into the lives of our descendants.

As we look forward, we must also look inward, recognizing that the journey of healing is as much about personal transformation as it is about collective change. It is about cultivating empathy for ourselves and those who came before us, understanding that they, too, were products of their time, often doing their best with the knowledge and resources available to them.

The horizon of possibility is not a distant dream but a tangible destination we can reach through conscious effort and societal commitment. It requires us to be both students and teachers, learning from the past and educating for the future. It asks us to be courageous, confront uncomfortable truths, and embrace the vulnerability that comes with genuine healing.

In this potential space, we find the seeds of a new narrative that honors our history without being hindered by it. It is a narrative that celebrates growth, champions resilience, and fosters a culture of emotional intelligence and psychological well-being.

As we close this chapter of our collective journey, let us implement the lessons learned optimistically. Let us commit to nurturing these seeds of possibility, watering them with our collective efforts, and watching as they blossom into a legacy of healing that will benefit future generations. The horizon is vast, and it is ours to shape.

What We Leave Behind

In the quiet afterglow of reflection, as we stand on the precipice of understanding and the dawn of healing, we are beckoned to consider the trajectory of our lives and the legacy we impart to those who follow. The journey through the pages of this exploration into inherited family trauma has been one of unraveling threads that weave through generations, binding us in a tapestry of shared history and collective memory.

We have delved into the shadows cast by our ancestors, not to dwell in the darkness but to bring light to the patterns that have shaped us. We have learned that trauma, when left unacknowledged, can echo through time, manifesting in the lives of those who were never present at its inception. Yet, with this knowledge comes a profound responsibility—a call to action that asks us to be the architects of a new legacy.

What we leave behind is a consequence of our actions and our conscious choices. It is a testament to the understanding that the wounds we heal in ourselves can mend fractures in the lineage we continue. As we step forward, let us do so to transform our inherited pain into wisdom, our silent struggles into dialogues of growth, and our healing into collective liberation.

To embark on this path requires courage—the courage to confront uncomfortable truths, to challenge long-held beliefs, and to open ourselves to the vulnerability of change. It demands that we be both students and teachers in life's lessons, recognizing that every interaction is an opportunity to either perpetuate cycles of suffering or foster cycles of healing.

Let us nurture resilience over resignation, empathy over apathy, and connection over isolation. In doing so, we honor those who came before us and those who will follow. Our actions today are the seeds of tomorrow's harvest, and it is within our power to cultivate a future where the legacy of trauma is replaced with triumph over adversity.

As we close this chapter of our collective journey, let us not forget that the story continues with each breath we take and every choice we make. The call to action is clear: to live with intention, to love with purpose, and to leave a legacy that echoes with the strength of healed hearts and the whispers of a brighter future for all who inherit the world we shape today.

Your Feedback Matters

As we reach the end of this book, I extend my heartfelt gratitude for your time and engagement. It's been an honor to share this journey with you, and I hope it has been as enriching for you as it has been for me.

If the ideas we've explored have sparked new thoughts, inspired change, or provided comfort, I'd really appreciate it if you could share your experience with others. Your feedback benefits me as an author and guides fellow readers in their quest for their next meaningful read.

To leave a review on Amazon, follow the QR code below. Your insights and reflections are invaluable; by sharing them, you contribute to a larger conversation that extends far beyond the pages of this book.

Thank you once again for your company on this literary adventure. May the insights you've gained stay with you, and may your continuous quest for knowledge be ever-fulfilling.

ABOUT THE AUTHOR

Essie Woodard is an author best known for her groundbreaking book series "Generational Healing." With a background in psychology and a passion for helping individuals break free from the chains of their past, Woodard has dedicated her career to exploring the complex realms of inherited family trauma and the challenges of dealing with emotionally immature parents. Her work offers insightful analysis, practical personal growth, and healing strategies, resonating with readers worldwide.

Made in United States
Orlando, FL
01 February 2024

43177530R00075